INDIAN MILITARY MEDICINE

VOLUME 3

Brigadier (Dr.) Yudhvir Suri, VSM

Published by Notion Press, 2025
Website: www.notionpress.com.
Email: notionpress.com
Author Name: Brigadier (Dr.) Yudhvir Suri, VSM
Copyright © Brigadier (Dr.) Yudhvir Suri, VSM
Title: Indian Military Medicine
All Rights Reserved.
ISBN
Paperback 979-8-89929-456-3
Hardcase 979-8-89929-457-0

Notion Press Pvt. Ltd.,

No: 50, Chettiyar Agaram Main Road,

Vanagaram,

Chennai- 600095,

Tamilnadu, India.

Printed by Notion Press Private Limited.
Made with ♥ on the Notion Press Platform

www.notionpress.com.

SOLDIER RELIGION

There are neither Hindus nor Muslims or minorities in Indian Army.

There are only soldiers, officers and other ranks with their surname. All celebrate festivals together. Officers lead the prayers, the faith of their troops, that is:

INDIAN ARMY

AND

SOLDIER RELIGION

"YUDHVIR SURI"

Those who walked on Pebble

Paved the way

Of future generations

Indian Military Medicine

Medical delivery to soldiers

Dedication

To those stress induced fixed gaze soldiers after-war

CONTENTS

1

INDIAN MILITARY MEDICINE

Indian Military Medicine can be looked as pre-World War I period, post-World War I to World War II and post-World War II.

1600–1857

- Pre-World War I

- East India Company and Mughal Empire.

1857–1942

- In between World War I and World War II – British India rule.

1947 onward

- Post-World War II, India Independence, 1947, Democratic Republic of India.

Post-World War II, India became independent from British colonial rule on 15th August, 1947.

Army Medical Corps, Armed Forces Medical Services were created exclusively to the medical care of the Indian soldiers.

The East India Company gave rudimentary soldier status and medical care to the Indian soldiers. They lacked sentiments, customs and traditions. Poor terms of service, pensions, promotion, increased cultural and social insensitivity from the British officers contributed to the feelings of discontent among the Indian soldiers of the Bengal Presidency Army. High Caste hindu sepoys felt as a threat to their traditional social status with recruitment to lower caste Hindus, Sikhs and Muslims. (General service enlistment Act on July 25, 1856) Tension eventually boiled over the introduction of the pattern 1853 Enfield rifle. Rumours quickly spread that the cartridges for the new rifle were greased with pig and cow fat, making them offensive to both Muslims and Hindus. Sepoys had to bite open the cartridge to liberate the powder in order to load the gun. There were existing concerns about the forced conversion to Christianity. On 29th March 1857, Sepoy Mangal Pandey of 34th Bengal Native Infantry at Barrackpore, North Calcutta, attacked his officers when his comrades were ordered to restrain him, they refused. But they stopped short of joining him in open revolt. It was handful of soldiers who were involved in the revolt but the entire regiment was disbanded in disgrace. Many soldiers thought this too harsh a punishment. The mutiny started in Meerut, near Delhi, on 10th May 1857. Eighty-five members of 3rd Bengal Light Cavalry who had been jailed for refusing to use rifle cartridges they believed to be at odds with their religion, were broken out of prison by their comrades. They ransacked the nearby military station killing the Europeans and Britishers. The situation rapidly escalated and spread, eventually involved all 10 of the Bengal light cavalry and most of its 74 native infantry regiments. Many units were disarmed. Thousands of common people joined the revolt, some for religious reasons, others for taxation and land policy. The outbreak at Meerut, uprisings by soldiers and civilians, happened across the northern and central India but the main centres of rebellion were Delhi, Kanpur, Lucknow, Jhansi and Gwalior. It was the biggest threat to British rule in the Indian subcontinent.

- Field Marshal Sir Colin Campbell: Commanded brigade in crimean war, Thin red line at Balaklava, later led a relief army with distinction during Indian mutiny of 1857.

- Major-General Robert Clive, secured India for Britain during Indian Mutiny of 1857.

1857, Bengal Army had 1,59,000 soldiers, 24,000 were Europeans and 1,35,000 were Indian sepoys (Infantry) and sowars (cavalry). The ratio was especially problematic in terms of discipline in the Bengal Presidency Army compared to other presidency armies of East India Company. This necessitated to reduce the number of British Army regiments in India. This was for reason of economy to send the soldiers to Crimean war (1854-1856).

1857 rebellion is also called the first war of Independence of India. Rebellion was resentments born of diverse perceptions but the ignition was the religious sentiment of the soldiers both the Hindus and Muslims. It was also the patriotic revolt against the British oppression. It led to the dissolution of East India Company and forced the British to reorganize the army, the financial system and the administration in India through the passage of the Government of India Act 1858. Thereafter, India was administered directly by the British Government as the new British Empire. On 01 November 1858, Queen Victoria issued a proclamation to Indians, which promised rights similar to those of other British citizens. However, this proclamation lacked the constitutional authority.

Administrator change from East India Company to Queen Victoria of British Empire started reforms to restructure the Army. It resulted in the break up of East India Company.

It impacted the career, life-style and medical care to the soldiers. The doors of military medical facilities were open with free access to the medical care to the Indian soldier.

Medical facilities exclusive to the British soldiers and European citizens at the three presidencies Bombay, Madras and Calcutta were converted to medical education institutes for Indian citizens.

There were 3,00,000 Indian sepoys enlisted to East India Company as opposed to 50,000 British prior to the uprising. It is estimated that 1,00,000 to 1,50,000 Indians were killed during the conflict in Oudh Lucknow region alone were civilians. There was massacre all over the country after the British forces took control of Delhi, Allahabad, Kanpur and Lucknow. Horrific British military action was the cruelty and public hanging to the rebels. General Neill committed disgraceful act of massacre of Indian civilians and the mutineers, and even those thought to be helping the uprising.

However, rebellion failed, East India Company dissolved, Queen Victoria took control of administration, reforms were instituted. Soldiers status was restored to the Indian soldiers. This was the first demarcation line to restore the status of Indian soldier.

India entered World War I on 5th August 1914, when British War Council in London decided that Indian Army would fight overseas. Indian Army fought against the German Empire, Egypt, Gallipoli, German, East Africa, Mesopotamia (the present day Iraq). Indian Army remained in war-mode till November 1918.

Lack of antibiotics hampered the survival rates especially the penetrating abdominal wounds. Anaesthesia, asepsis antisepsis, surgical skills and wound management permitted surgery of seriously wounded and complex injuries with high survival of the wounded soldiers. Development of lethal weapons and explosives was seen with parallel development of scientific management of anaesthesia, surgery, wound care, prostheses, critical care and rehabilitation. The advances in medical care allowed the patients to survive.

Concept of forward field management was evolved to care the sick and wounded. Frontline regimental medical officers were posted and the experienced were assigned to manage the serious at the rear medical facility.

World War 1 evolved the concept of staging medical care.

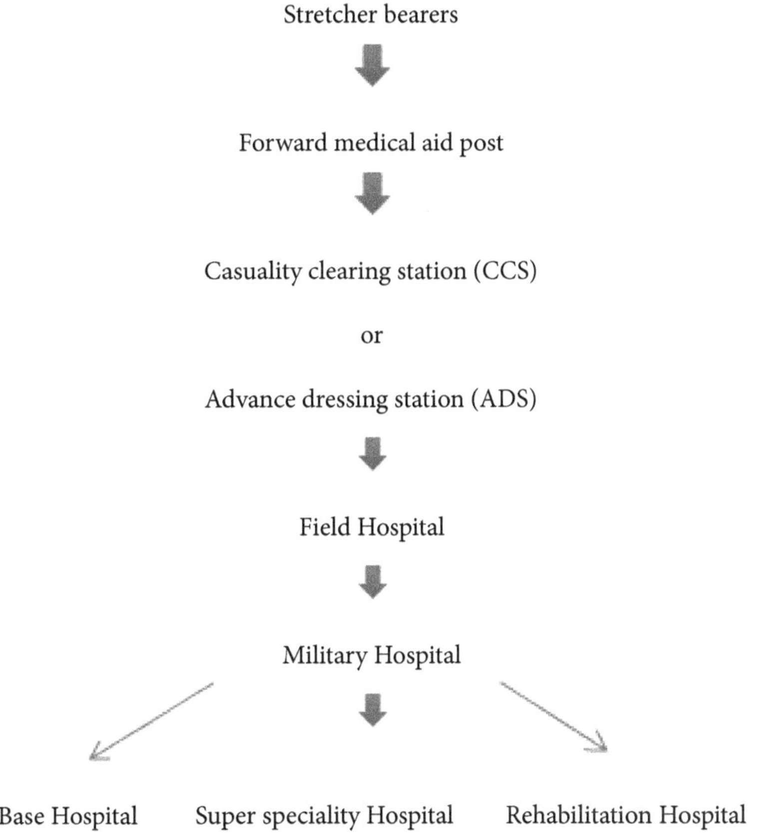

It was an organised medical care service, unlike in the past, to save limbs and life of the soldiers. Military forward medical management, rapid transportation and good nursing attributed to reduce mortality of the battle casualties.

First time in the history of military medicine, **"Time-factor", early to care** the wounded had dramatic improvement in survival. Early debridement of the wounds eliminated the gas-gangrene. Tetanus vaccine eliminated the tetanus disease amongst the wounded soldiers. Military nursing service, trained and partially trained volunteers significantly altered the scenario to benefit the seriously wounded soldiers. Newly developed insecticides DDT, personal hygiene, environmental sanitation controlled the infectious diseases such as typhus, scarlet, trench fever, malaria, diarrhoea, dysentery and typhoid.

World War II was seen of triage rapid transport, management of shock, blood transfusion, control of infectious diseases, aviation and submarine medicine. Injectable morphine became the wonder-drug to reduce pain and shock during evacuation. Organised stages of medical care of sick and wounded was the standard adopted in the army. Antibiotics turned the history of military medicine in care of critically wounded penetrating battlefield trauma. Forward field surgery was accepted norm to save the limb and life of the soldier.

Post World War II, was the transition of consolidation and amalgamation of medical manpower and infrastructure of medical delivery to the soldier. Those commissioned in the Indian Medical Service of the British Indian Army were seconded to Army Medical Corps, that was created exclusively to medical care of the Indian soldiers. Lieutenant General Kekharsee Sorabji Master, MC who was granted King George Commission as the rank of captain on 01 April, 1927 became the first Director General Armed Forces Medical Services in the rank as Lieutenant General on 15th August, 1947. This is an important link of medical manpower-infrastructure consolidation of pre and post independent India.

POST-INDEPENDENCE:

Army Medical Corps, post-independence has travelled 75 years, excellent brains of military medical leadership proved. "Those who walked on pebbles, paved the way of future generations", to deliver to the Indian soldier. Many such military medical leaders, "Took over empty Patanjali Bowl, handed over nectar full Dhanvantari Bowl; the best example is General Sorabji Master. Those days, medical graduate (MBBS) was considered high qualification, that too, was in short supply. There were five basic specialities of medical sciences- General medicine, General Surgery, Anaesthesiology, diagnostics-laboratory and imaging (pathology and radiology) and preventive medicine contrary to the present day 37 specialities of medicine, super specialities and super-subspecialities. Army Medical Corps has committed comprehensive medical care to the soldiers, veterans and families. However, war surgery and medicine cannot be compromised, therefore, specialists and super-specialists must be trained and prepared to serve in the forward lethal zones of hostilities during war and peace. Super-specialists must provide their services to the basic specialities of surgery and medicine during hostilities.

BASE HOSPITAL CONCEPT

After the World War I and II, there was need to build Army Base Hospitals, to accommodate the wounded soldiers returning from abroad. These soldiers needed surgery and rehabilitation. Army Base hospitals were also required to the needs of the local troops, veterans and families. Facilities at the base hospitals were state-of-the-art comprehensive health care to the soldier. Base Hospital infrastructure is differentiated as higher than the military hospital but not comparable to Army referral and research teaching medical college, that should be understood at command and lower leadership level.

The role of base hospital is different than the model of Army referral and research teaching hospital, as seen at Delhi Cantt. Base hospitals were designed to move with the strength of the troops. Each base hospital is authorized a mobile surgical unit, infrastructure is usually unutilised in the modern warfare. Brig Yudhvir Suri, (then Lieutenant Colonel) had laid the demonstration of mobile surgical unit of 92 base hospital, Srinagar Kashmir.

Army base hospital was located at Delhi Cantt Sadar Bazar, sometime, after the World War 1. The old mule-animal barracks were converted to the medical indoor facility. Military leadership decided to move the Base hospital to its present location of old army hospital complex at Brar-Square Delhi Cantt in 1996. Army hospital referral and research had moved to its new multi-storey complex at Subroto Park, Dhaula Kuan New Delhi. It appears to be a penny-save economy decision of the administration. The perpetual old infrastructure problems were transferred from Army to Base hospital, those problems exist, further, it has added the horse-stud OPD complex, to the dislike of the soldiers.

What soldier looks, when he visits the medical facility? Infrastructure and hassle free access to the medical care. He fails to penetrate inside the excellent brain workforce of the doctors. 2019-2021 was the worst national Covid calamity. Base Hospital Delhi was declared as the nodal Covid-centre to manage the soldiers, veterans and families. Government of India opened the doors of military hospitals to civilians. Unprecedented unethical decision at the cost of precious lives of the soldiers. (Abrupt transfer of Army Base Hospital commandant Major General Vasu Vardhan, raised eyebrows, Times of India May 12, 2021.) Base Hospital medical facility was increased from 450 beds to 1000 beds. Brig Yudhvir Suri, VSM (then Colonel) was offg Commandant 1999-2000, more than one year, awaiting to pickup the next higher rank. Some lessons were learnt during this period:

- Do not preach religion within the hospital complex. Designated areas to be used for social religious function.

- Do not permit indoor soldiers (patients) as sevadars, cooks, working and ward labour work community service may be permitted to facilitate comrade physical and emotional health recovery.

- Do not permit indoor soldiers for even menial self purpose.

- Military medical leadership to remain alert, keep lower echelon alert to facilitate medical delivery to the soldiers on daily basis.

- Military Medical leadership is responsible to all comfort to the soldier within the hospital complex.

Soldiers do not compare the service hospital with corporate medical facility. However, it is the responsibility of the military leadership, medical and non-medical, to provide comparable medical standards professional as well as the comfort facilities.

Example: Visit the corporate hospital, one is greeted, do you need wheelchair? Voluntary service free of cost. In service hospital, administration has provided the car-connectivity within the hospital complex, emergency to pharmacy and so on, but lacks the spirit of those who are detailed to work. This spirit needs to be activated on daily basis by the local military leadership.

Indian military medicine is committed to the soldier. Knowledge, skill and art of medicine of civil experts are translated to the soldier. War medicine and surgery is innovated and modified to the needs of the soldier. Cardiothoracic and Vascular medicine as the super-speciality culture in armed forces is the example. Military hospital Aundh near Kirkee Pune was created for the comprehensive tuberculosis management after the World War II. It had the distinction of pulmonary surgery, probably, first time in India, to the soldiers. Tuberculosis destroyed lung, non-treatable with medicines, was submitted to surgery as the cure life saving. Tuberculosis management was the need of that time to the soldier. Designation of military hospital Aundh Kirkee Pune was changed as the cardiothoracic centre and shifted to Golibar maidan, associated teaching hospital, Armed Forces Medical College, Pune, sometime early 1960s. That was the time cardiac surgery open heart had started in the civil medical facilities in India. Surgeons experimented in the animal laboratory operation theatre, learn and adopted on human, in hospital operation theatre, was the start. It was seen at AIIMS New Delhi and cardiothoracic centre Pune almost parallel progress. Lieutenant General (then colonel) A M Ahuja was the first to repair the atrial septal defect on cardiac bypass on 12 February 1969 and later ventricular septal defect in 1972. Cardiothoracic centre Pune was established as the nodal cardiac centre including cardiology and pulmonary medicine with illustrious surgeons, cardiologists, chest physicians (later called pulmonary critical care physicians), anaesthesiologists and trained nurses. Brigadier Radhakrishnan Sundara Rajan (then Colonel) was the first to perform coronary artery bypass surgery in 1994. Armed Forces Medical Services decided to expand the cardiothoracic vascular medicine and surgery sciences to deliver to the soldier at the doorsteps of the command and zonal hospitals in the country. It started with the cardiology centres with the posting of cardiologists later developed cardiothoracic - cardiac surgeon, anaesthesiologists, critical care specialists and trained cardiac OT nurses. Since these hospitals had become the teaching recognised DNB post graduate institutes, therefore, it was the need of time to start cardiothoracic centres. Cardiothoracic Pune, besides open heart surgery, had distinction of close-heart (mitral valvotomy, pulmonary ductus anomaly and other congenital cardiac disorder) and pulmonary surgery to benefit the soldier, veterans and families.

Lieutenant General SK Kaul (the Colonel) was the first to be posted at Army Hospital referral and research on 1st July 1997 followed by Air Marshal Dipankar Ganguli (then Colonel) who were responsible to the expansion of Cardiothoracic Vascular surgery with functioning from the new Cardiothoracic building block at AHRR on 1st January 2015. Further CTVS centres have been established at Calcutta, Bangalore, Ashwini, Delhi and Pune with modern infrastructure. Delhi AHRR and Pune AICTVS are the largest nodal cardiovascular and thoracic centres of Armed Forces Medical Services in India. Both these centres are commanded by the cardiac surgeons with the rank as Brigadier. 30th November 2024, Brigadier Yudhvir Suri, VSM author of this book Indian Military Medicine Volume 3 visited the CTVS-AHRR and posed a question to Brigadier Jaswinder Singh, an eminent cardiothoracic surgeon HOD, why the word "Advanced" – Dept. of Advanced cardiothoracic surgery & Heart and lung transplantation - depicted outside. He replied,

- Largest cardiothoracic centre of Armed Forces Medical Services, 800-900 cardiac, 50-60 pulmonary surgery every year.

- Cardiac surgery on beating heart.

- Minimal invasive cardiac surgery without sternotomy on bypass.

- Paediatric Complex congenital heart surgeries about 100 cases every year.

- Cardiac transplant, first heart transplant was done at CTVS-AHRR by Lieutenant General Manoj Luthra (then Colonel) on 30 August 2007. So far 28 cardiac transplant surgeries have been done with significant post survival period (80% had more than 5 years post survival). Cardiac team has a significant waiting of the transplant patients. It is interesting to mention that Brigadier Sameer Kumar, another eminent cardiac surgeon at AICTVS Pune has also done cardiac transplant surgery in a paediatric patient in 2022. Why the name cardiothoracic centre - CTC Pune? is changed to Army Institute of Cardiothoracic and Vascular Sciences, probably, budget allocation, ministry of defence, medical Directorate DGAFMS, New Delhi. However, it remains the premier medical educational facility to the graduates, postgraduates, nursing and paramedicals of Armed Forces Medical Service. It is an infrastructure asset to train the future generation of medical manpower.

- Extracorporeal Membrane Oxygenator (ECMO) facility at CTVS - AHRR since 2015.

- Those trained as cardiothoracic surgeons are the potential excellent war surgeons with expertise of vascular anastomosis that can reduce the incidence of limb-loss in vascular trauma in battle - casualties.

- Indian military medicine, suggest to train the general surgeons as graded specialists of cardiothoracic surgery exclusively for the purpose of war-surgery with due training and curriculum.

- Armed forces medical service needs the basic war medicine and surgery specialists. Manpower and infrastructure should always be prepared to the cause of nation.

Personal Communication –

Brigadier Radhakrishnan Sundara Rajan, VSM

Brigadier Jaswinder Singh

Brigadier Sameer Kumar

Lieutenant General Manoj Luthra, VSM

SOLDIER NEEDS NEW MEDICAL TRENDS -----

There is dynamic changing trend of medical care since World War I and World War II, expanding super specialities of specific medical fields, super-subspecialities and critical care. Emergency medicine and critical care have evolved as the separate decision making medical specialties.

Army Medical Corps has evolved 100% specialists medical manpower corps. DGMO is the terminology of the past. Study leave to the medical officers is more liberal, to have the speciality of their choice from civil medical universities in India.

Armed Forces Medical Services of India has been following the trends of medical care to the soldier but much needs to be done:

- **MO specialists or non-degree holder "graded specialists" do not stand legal validity. It needs constitutional nod of parliament even during the hostilities or emergency. Soldier needs qualified experienced expert medical hands to care them.**

- Critical Care has evolved in specific fields of medicine, even superspecialities have expanded to the critical care. Specialists of various fields of medicine need to opt for training such as:

Multispecialty critical care	Anaesthesiologists.
Paediatrics Neonatology critical care	Paediatricians.
Respiratory critical care	Pulmonologists Anaesthesiologists.
Neurology critical care and rehabilitation	Neurologists
Cardiac care critical care	Cardiologists
Post-Cardiac Surgery critical care	Cardiothoracic Surgeons
Traumatology critical care	Surgeons, Anaesthesiologists

Therefore, administration needs to set the targets of adequate numbers of critical case specialists in each field based on the number of beds at each medical facility. One speciality to care all critical care of various fields of medicine will be mismatched to the standards of medical care.

- Emergency medicine is another field of decision-making. That needs to be adopted in Armed Forces Medical Services, India. Duty medical officer culture (DMO) of rotational medical field specialists is outdated. It needs to be revolutionalised with the induction, training and infrastructure of emergency medicine. It needs organisation reforms at the military medical leadership. AFMC to initiate advance course curriculum of grading and post-graduation at Pune University. Emergency medicine trained manpower will be resource reserve of war medicine at the forward lethal zone. It will facilitate forward field management of battle-casualties. It will reduce mortality, morbidity, hospitalisation and revenue saving to the state. Military medicine suggest mini critical care indoor model with monitoring, diagnostic facilities, dieted nursing care units at the command, zonal and military hospitals. Soldier looks at the civil medical facilities and expect the same standards from the Armed Forces Medical Services to the troops, veterans and families.

- **Critical care is specific to the field of medicine.** Training in specific speciality such as neuro-anaesthesia, paediatric anaesthesia does not fulfill the requirement of neuro-critical care or paediatric critical care specialists. It needs fellowship or degree training of specific critical care field at the recognised medical institute or university.

INSTITUTION OF REGIMENTAL MEDICAL OFFICER:

Army Medical Corps has strengthened the institution of regimental medical officer by creating the best Laishram Jyoti Singh, Ashok Chakra field events trophy at the MOBC level at Army Medical Corps Centre and College Lucknow. First time brave-hearts who sacrificed to the cause of the Nation have been instituted by the Medical Corps, is appreciated. There are many, professional medical scholars, medical specialities and superspecialities, who contributed and delivered to the soldier. Many have earned distinguished service medals, Vir Chakras and Mahavir Chakras in Army Medical Corps that will be remembered by Indian Military Medicine History.

MAJOR LEISHRAM JYOTI SINGH, ASHOK CHAKRA, CITATION AND STORY:

Major Leishram Jyoti Singh was born on 14th May 1972 at Nambol Awang Lekai, a small town in Manipur. His father, Laishram Markando Singh was a state government agriculture-horticulture employee and mother, Laishram Ibeyama Devi was home-maker. He did his initial schooling from Manipur (Boys) Public School (MPS) and known by the nick name "Ibungo". He was diligent, conscientious, punctual and athlete sportsman.

He did his MBBS from Regional Institute of Medical Sciences (RIMS) Imphal in 1996. His passion for sports brought him to pursue post-graduation in sports medicine from Netaji Subhas National Institute of Sports in 2001, at Patiala.

Self-disciplined, hard-working, doctor from North-East region who struggled hard during his young days of education decided to join Armed Forces Medical Services of India. He was commissioned into Army Medical Corps (AMC) on 15th February 2003. He did his Medical Officers Basic Course (MOBC) at Officers Training School, AMC Centre and College Lucknow. Young civilian doctor was turned to gentleman soldier, doctor and dedicated patriot officer of the Indian Army. He was posted as Regimental Medical officer Border Roads organisation Arunachal Pradesh in High-Altitude. He also served at Military Hospital Agartala. He represented Army Medical Corps at World Military Games 2007 at Hyderabad, common-wealth games 2008 to provide medical cover for one of the disciplines at Pune.

December 2009, he was posted to Indian Medical Mission Afghanistan. On 26 February 2010, at Kabul, at 0630 am, three burkha clad terrorists and a driver tried to drive their car past the concrete barrier placed at the entrance to the Noor Guest House in the Shar E Naw an upscale place in Kabul where Jyotin and other Indian staff were lodged. The neighbouring guest house had other international guests. Afghan security guards and private armed security personnels challenged the car, three of the terrorists alighted and rushed away. The driver detonated the car and himself about 60 meters short of the entrance to the guest houses. The blast left a 12 feet wide and 6 feet deep crater.

Two terrorists entered the neighbouring guest house. The third terrorist (whose Joridar had blown himself up with the car bomb) rushed into the Noor guest house. All the four terrorists were explosive laden suicide vests. Those of the two terrorists who rushed to the neighboring guest house, one of them blew himself up with the suicide vest. The other escaped from the blast hole in the wall.

The terrorist who entered the Noor guest house, searching the Hindi speaking residents and guests. This terrorist found himself standing in front of the door of Major Laishram Jyotin Singh with an AK-47 assault rifle in his hand. He had probably exhausted his grenades.

Laishram Jyotin Singh, standing face to face with the courier of death itself, clad in a deadly suicide vest who was about to lift his AK-47 rifle for a deathly sweep in front of him. The next rooms, a few feet away were occupied by the other Indian officials, officers, colleagues who too were unarmed as per diplomatic protocol and agreements with the Afghanistan government, Major Jyotin had instinctive response, no time for thinking about actions and reactions, split second action driven by the desire and mental focus to save lives. The sportsman doctor triggered the automotor action to react in the best possible defensive manner. Major Jyotin Singh pounced upon the terrorist standing just a foot or two away from him. The terrorist dropped the assault rifle on being surprised by this most unexpected reaction of the gallant doctor and wrestled with Jyotin. In desperation, the terrorist detonated the suicide vest that he was wearing. In milliseconds, the bodies were blown into smithereens by the powerful RDX. Young Major Laishram Jyotin Singh, 38 years, sacrificed himself to save the killings and annihilation that the terrorist would have brought upon others in the guest rooms. He died a heroic death.

Major (Dr.) Laishram Jyotin Singh was awarded the Ashok Chakra, the highest peace-time gallantry award in the Indian Armed Forces on 26 January 2011, the first army doctor to get the highest peace-time gallantry award.

Army Medical Corps, men and officers, are proud of Major Jyotin's sacrifice to the Nation, President of India, Pratibha Patil, handed over the award to Laishram Boeing Singh, younger brother of Major (Dr) Laishram Jyotin Singh on Republic Day 26th January, 2011.

- MS-14522 F (Short Service Commission) MR-08609 M (Permanent Commission) Army Medical Corps (AMC) Armed

Forces Medical Services India. Ashok Chakra (equivalent to Mahavir Chakra of Indian Army)

REGIMENTAL MEDICAL OFFICER:

Regimental Medical Officer is posted to the fighting unit for a tenure of 2-3 years but remains enlisted to their strength life-long. He learns the soldier life-style, grooms with the soldiers as military way of life, permanent relationship grows for generations to remember. Many of us are invited to their "Unit Honours day" or celebrations of the Unit functions. Ex-RMO Brigadier (then Captain)

Yudhvir Suri who served the Deccan Horse (9-Horse) armoured Corps 1970-1972 at Chhamb - Jaurian (J&K) was invited as "guest of Honour" on 14th September 2024 at JV Day (Jordan Valley Day) Celebrations located somewhere in Rajasthan. 55 years had gone down the history, relationship was respect, hospitality, cordiality and humility from officers, Junior Commissioned officers, other ranks and families of the regiment.

Post 1971 hostilities at Chhamb-Jaurian, was the critical time of anxiety to the families of brave soldiers. HQS permitted the families for a limited period of 5-7 days at the forward location. During this period, sometime August 1972, after the ceasefire, young bachelors officers presented beautifully crafted invitations to the ladies camped in the tentage accommodation at the forward location of the regiment. Mrs. Suri was one of them. That invitation, 55 years preserved document, was presented to the regiment as "war memorial family welfare momento" to be preserved in the Regiment diary.

Regiment diary is the History document that reveals the events held during that period. Colonel Sudarshan Commandant presented the interesting write-up of the diary of the regiment 1970-1972.

Birth of Munir Suri, younger son of Ex-RMO Brigadier Yudhvir Suri, VSM was recorded and read over to the officer during this visit on 15 September 2024 at Comdts office.

Brigadier Yudhvir Suri Health trophy depicting "Patanjali with bowl of nectar", Healthy soldiers, Health of the Unit, is the fighting spirit to win the war was presented to the commandant and all ranks of the regiment.

Ex-RMO Brigadier Yudhvir Suri was presented a prestigious Deccan Horse momento by the Commandant that depicts the War-History of the regiment from the days of Royal Deccan Horse of 1st world war.

Brigadier Yudhvir Suri, VSM served the regiment from 1970 to 1972 and fought 1971 Chhamb-Jaurian war as regimental medical officer. In memory of that silvo-salvo was presented to the officers mess.

Bara-khana was an occasion to meet the junior commissioned officers and other rank soldiers. It was an interesting interaction with them to find high morale fighting spirit and addressed them to convey our gratitude — once RMO always RMO of the regiment.

Ladies Welfare: It is interesting to document that the present day soldier's wives are highly educated, many of them are post-graduates, skillful and talented. It was wonderful traditional welcome to Mrs Suri, probably life-time experience as guest of honour to the regiment.

It was a privilege and honor to pray for the welfare of the soldiers, families and veterans of the regiment as "guest of honor" — honor bestowed to the Ex-RMO of the regiment — at mandir and gurudwara of the regiment, along with officers, JCOs, other ranks and families.

Soldier needs medical officer at the backyard during the war and at the doorstep during the peace. Solution is the regimental medical officer. Medical and non-medical military leadership need to ensure it Army Medical Corps need to strengthen the post and status of the regimental medical officer. Indian Military Medicine will endorse those who serve the soldier at the forward lethal zone of hostility borders.

2

CONTRIBUTORS TO THE EXCELLENCE

Military Surgeon Lieutenant General Kekhasree Sorabji Master, MC.

Physician – Administrator

Armed Forces Medical Services, India.

Born in Bombay on 21st January 1891. He belonged to Parsi community, who had migrated as Persian refugees to British ruled India. He had early education in Bombay, then secured admission to the field of his choice Medicine. Licentiate Medicine (LM) was the curriculum of 3 years at selective Medical Institutes in India during pre – independence period. Kekhasree secured admission at Dublin, the capital city of the Republic of Ireland, then the settlement of British Empire.

- Sushil Talwar: Indian recipients of Military Cross Volume I and Volume II, Alok Books distributors ISBN – 10 – 93863 – 88702 – pg 112 – 113.

  Lieutenant General, Surname is spelt "Kekhasree" Vide IALS upto 1924, thereafter, "Kekhasru"

- *The name indicates that the family migrated from Central Asia, north – eastern Iran, where it constitutes modern "Khorasan" province, part of north – west Afghanistan and three Asian republics Tajikistan, Turkmenistan and Uzbekistan, earst while, Russian territory, now independent states.*

  He completed diploma Medicine (Licentiate Medicine (LM) sometime mid - 1914, the first World War, was the need of British India – Indian Medical Service that he joined on 10th August, 1915 in the rank as temporary Lieutenant, promoted to the rank as temporary Captain till 10th February, 1927.

- *Temporary rank Lieutenant, Captain or Major was the symbol of status, equality to other arms and service, and pay remuneration without the name in the London Gazette notification.*

  During this period, August 1915 to January 1920, he participated at the war of Mesopotamia – present day Iraq including Turkie, Syria and Kuwait. It was World War I conflict between British Empire and Ottoman Turks (now Iraq).

War Allies

UK, India, Australia, New Zealand, Kuwait and Assyrian Volunteers

Vs

Ottoman Empire (Iraq), Germany, Arab tribes, Kurdish tribes, Al – Munta fiq Union.

Mesopotamia campaign started 6th November, 1914 till 14th November, 1918 (4 years 1 week 01 day),

There were 85, 000 British Allies battle – wounded casualties and 1, 54, 343 evacuated as sick of disease (Total 2, 56, 000 causalities). General Kekhasree was awarded Mention – in – dispatch twice to honour his distinguished service to the sick and wounded.

The officer held the rank as temporary Captain, the honour and award was not London Gazette notification record.

Except third time mention – in – dispatch as Lieutenant Colonel on 23rd December, 1943duly signed by the secretary of state of war.

General Kekhasree was awarded Military Cross, equivalent to Maha – Vir Chakra of post – independence India, during the same period of lethal war zone, on 18th January, 1918.

His gallant deed was to rescue, evacuate, and salvage 1790 casualties on the ship Vasana, a transport ship that was converted as a hospital 613 beds with 125 hospital staff as an ambulance transport to the sick and wounded. His military cross was forwarded to war office of India vide receipts of Military Cross by Indian (Sushil Talwar, page 113)

After World War I; Kekhasee Sorabji master, MC was posted to Rawalpindi, Jabalpur, and Bombay as Regimental Medical Officer between 1920 – 1928. During this period, he persued to complete his graduation in Medicine (MBBS) from Grant Medical College Mumbai.

- Grant Medical College, Mumbai was started in 1845. LSLM (Licentiate Medicine) qualified doctors were discontinued from the Armed Forces India Aras it chartered MBBS as the basic qualification Army Medical Corps, 1943. However, LSLM qualified were allowed the option of two years curriculum at various Medical Colleges in India to qualify MBBS.

General Kekharsee Sorabji Master MC, was granted King George Commission as the rank of Captain on 01st April, 1927.

- *A commission is a formal document issued to appoint a named person to high office or a commissioned officer in a territory's armed forces. It is a document authority that a person named is vested with the powers of that office and is empowered to execute official acts.*

Since 1915 till 1927, General KS Master, MC was awarded King's Commission first time in British India Armed Forces as Indian citizen in Indian Medical Service in 1927 (document reproduced) that was recorded London Gazette notification. However, service for pay, pension and promotion was carried as the war period service, the officer had delivered to the sick and wounded WEF 1915.

During World War II, General master, MC again served in the middle – east, first as Commanding Officer 16 Indian General Hospital, then Assistant Director Medical Services (ADMS) 6 IndianDivision and PAI forces.

- *Persia and Iraq Force (PAI) was deployed as British ally force against the Rashid Ali at Gaylani Iraq, ally force (Anglo – Iraqi War, 1941).*

Press information Bureau, defence wing document that General master served in various capacities in North – Western Frontier and Waziristan (now in Pakistan), the major port of his career was to deliver to the sick and wounded in the War Zones.

Lieutenant General Master, MC remains an important link of Indian Medical Service of pre – independence and post – independence India. He was appointed as director medical services, Lahore district, that was a civil designation, in1944.

- *Indian Medical Service, in British India, served during the two World War (World War I & World War II). It remained in existence, until 1947, independence of India. Many of the officers who were both Indian and British have served in civil hospitals, to mention a few are*

  ▲ *Sir Ronald Ross (Noble prize)*

  ▲ *Sir Benjamin Franklin (physician to Monarchies)*

  ▲ *Sir Henry Vandyke Carter (Gray's anatomy fame)*

  ▲ *General Master and many others of Indian Medical Service served the military as well as the civil establishments of those days.*

General Master had the distinction to be appointed as Hon'y physician to His Majesty King George of United Kingdom, in 1944. Later in 1946, he was appointed as the Deputy Director Medical Services (DDMS) Northern Command in the rank of Major – General.

- **15th August, 1947, he became the first Director – General Armed Forces Medical Services India in the rank as Lieutenant general.**

- He integrated the amalgamated pre – independence medical services to Army Medical Corps to strengthen the infrastructure of medical care of the Army, Navy and Airforce.

- His expert administrative skills of medical delivery system was excellent to deliver the soldier during 1947 – 48 Indo – Pak War Kashmir.

- **Two – third of his medical career was spent in the lethal War Zones.**

During pre – independence Indian Medical Service (1915 – 1943) and immediately after the take – over as DGAFMS (1947 – 1948) Indo – Pak Kashmir.

Military Medicine will remember Lieutenant General KS Master, MC as the "Medical General of War Services". Of India.

- Lieutenant General KS Master, MC created resources of manpower and infrastructure of medical services to benefit the soldier in peace and war.

- **Lieutenant General KS Master, MC took over the Empty Patanjali Bowl and Handed – over the Nectar Full Dhanvantari Bowl of health immortality to the future generation of soldiers in India that will be remembered in Indian Military Medicine.**

- Lieutenant General KS Master, MC retired on October 1st, 1950 after 35 years of distinguished service to the Armed forces Medical Services India.

- *Colonel Saurab Bhardwaj, VSM, AHQs MPRSO Division personnel communication.*

- *United Service India (USI), library and research.*

- *Press information Bureau, Defence Wing memorandum Defence Service Medical Chief retired in01 October, 1950*

- *King George commission Captain Kekhasree Sorabji Master 01 April, 1927*

- *Honour and Award Mention – in – dispatch Lieutenant Colonel KS Master,MC, 28th December, 1943 London Gazette.*

- **Based on research by Team Indian Military Medicine.**

- **MPRSO did not exist when Lieutenant General KS Master, MC retired**

- Brigadier Yudhvir Suri, VSM: In Indian Military Medicine, Volume 2, Pg 182 – 183, 2024, Zorba books Pvt. Ltd. Gurugram.

Military medical leadership

Took over

Empty Patanjali Bowl

39

Handed over

Nectar full Dhanvantari Bowl

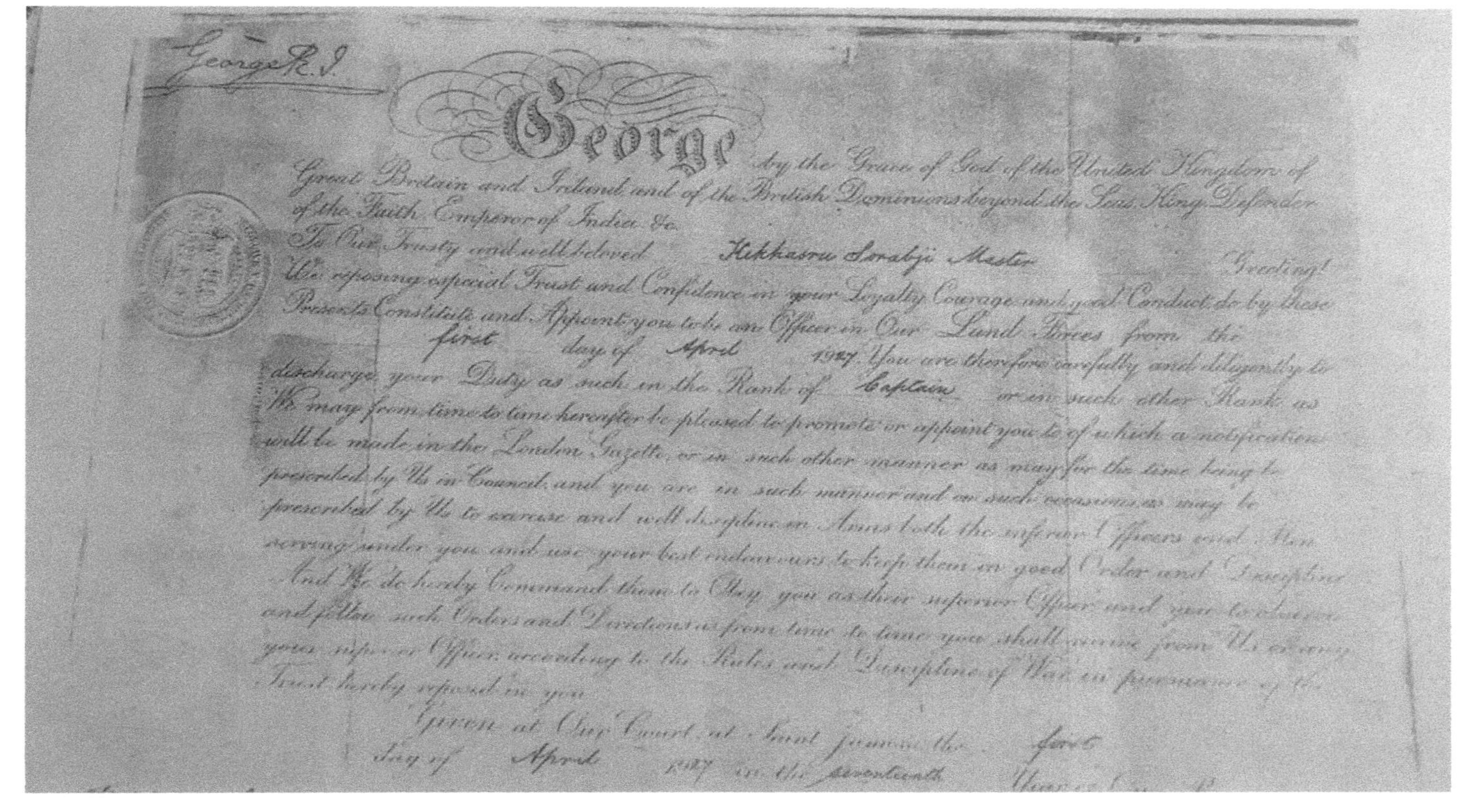

George R.I.

George by the Grace of God of the United Kingdom of Great Britain and Ireland and of the British Dominions beyond the Seas King Defender of the Faith, Emperor of India &c.

To Our Trusty and well beloved   Hikkasru Sorabji Master   Greeting!

We reposing especial Trust and Confidence in your Loyalty Courage and good Conduct do by these Presents Constitute and Appoint you to be an Officer in Our Land Forces from the   first   day of   April   1927. You are therefore carefully and diligently to discharge your Duty as such in the Rank of   Captain   or in such other Rank as We may from time to time hereafter be pleased to promote or appoint you to of which a notification will be made in the London Gazette, or in such other manner as may for the time being be prescribed by Us in Council and you are in such manner and on such occasions as may be prescribed by Us to exercise and well discipline in Arms both the inferior Officers and Men serving under you and use your best endeavours to keep them in good Order and Discipline And We do hereby Command them to Obey you as their superior Officer and you to observe and follow such Orders and Directions as from time to time you shall receive from Us or any your superior Officer according to the Rules and Discipline of War in pursuance of the Trust hereby reposed in you

Given at Our Court at Saint James the   first   day of   April   1927 in the seventeenth Year of Our Reign

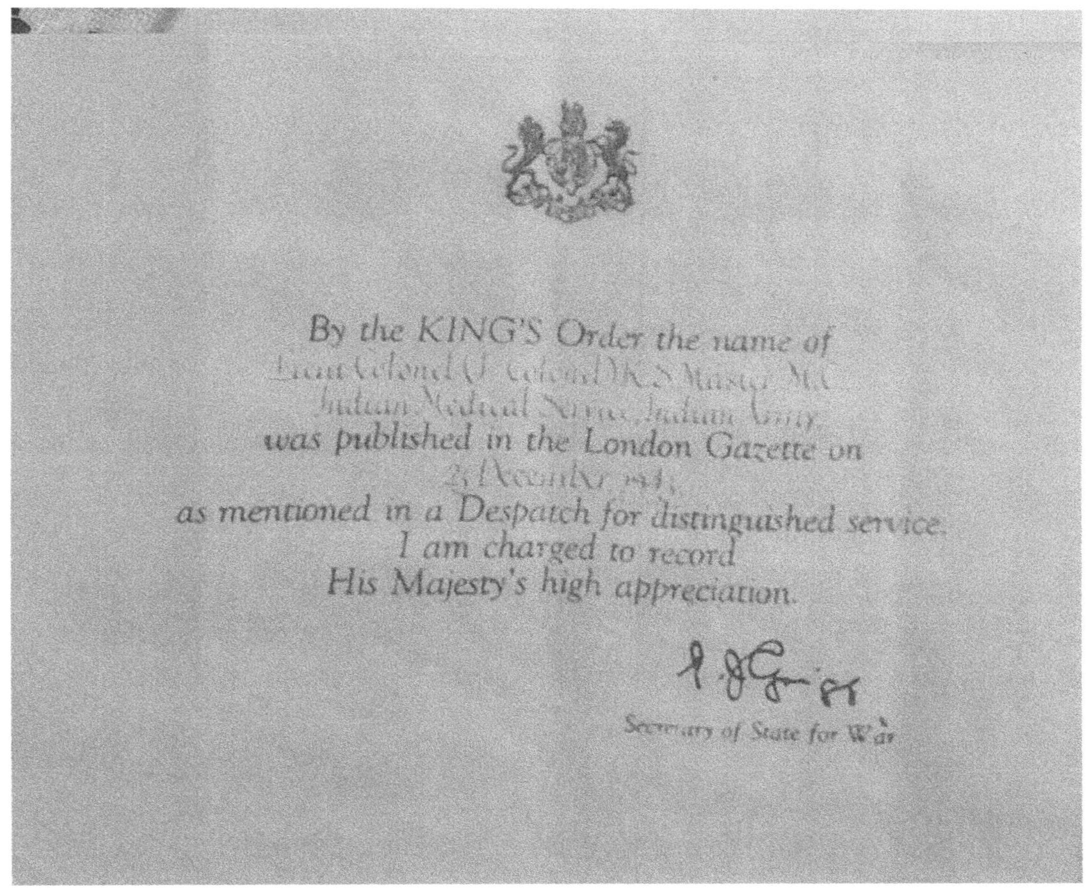

By the KING'S Order the name of
Lieut Colonel (A/Colonel) K. S. Master M.C.
Indian Medical Service, Indian Army,
was published in the London Gazette on
2 December 1943,
as mentioned in a Despatch for distinguished service.
I am charged to record
His Majesty's high appreciation.

Secretary of State for War

Military Surgeon

Air Marshal

Surender Kumar Bhalla

Cardiothoracic Anesthesiologist

Armed Forces Medical Services,

India

Air Marshal Surender Kumar Bhalla was born on 11th February, 1929. His father late Shri Hukam Chand Bhalla was a doctor – medical practioner at Jalandhar (Punjab). He studied initial education in DAV School Jalandhar, topped in matriculation, persued inter – science (medical) to become a doctor – it was an early decision. Those days to become a doctor, it was necessary to opt for medical after matriculation at inter – science medical level. He secured admission in the prestigious Lahore Medical college for graduation in medicine. 1947, partition of India, Air Marshal Surender Kumar Bhalla, had to shift to Andhra Medical College, Vishakhapatnam, to complete the last two years of medicine (MBBS) in 1950.

Air Marshal Surender Kumar Bhalla was commissioned into the Army Medical Corps (AMC) on 01st June, 1951 and superannuated on 31st August, 1988 as a Director General Medical Service, Airforce (DGMS – Air). He did his internship training at Airforce hospital Bangalore, promoted to Flt. Lt. on 01st June, 1952.

He served as Regimental Medical Officer to various Airforce fighting squadrons from 1952 to 01st December, 1959 till he achieved the rank as Squadron Leader in Airforce (equivalent to Major in Army).

Air Marshal Surender Kumar Bhalla had special interest in Anesthesiology as early as 1950. He did his diploma anesthesia (DA) and doctorate in Medicine – anesthesiology (MD anesthesiology) from Delhi University. He is the only person to have got distinction in MD from Delhi University. Those days there were eminent recognized teachers at different Medical Institutes in Delhi including Army Hospital. These teachers conducted the combined teaching programme under the ageisis of the university. Those registered under recognized teacher's of the university were conducted combined postgraduation to award the degree of MD from Delhi University. AFMC did not have the "grading" courses for diploma anesthesia of one year till early 1960. First batch of 2 years advance course in anesthesia for "grading" and MD Pune University was started in 1972.

Air Marshal Surender Kumar Bhalla had the true spirit of – "knowledge, art of skill, and practice" of the specialty. He worked during the critical time of China aggression 1962 to manage large number of high – altitude and battle casualties at Army Hospital, Delhi. It was first time military medicine had learnt the high – altitude disease. His experimental hemodynamic shock study postulated the administration of blood, colloid and crystalloid in the ratio of 1:2:3 has been the standard of shock management till today. He was the confidence of the surgeons to operate critical war trauma patients that was considered inoperable earlier. His research on Electro – Anesthesia was a new dimension in anesthesiology. Critical care became the superspeciality of anesthesiology with two beds for high – altitude disease at Army hospital (RR) in 1962 with research, understanding and management by Air Marshal Bhalla and team. It was the first concept of critical care in India.

1966, he was posted to AFMC as a member of faculty to train "specialist – anesthesia" grading medical officers, many of them were registered and qualified Diploma Anesthesia from Pune University. In 1971, Air Marshal Bhalla had cardiothoracic anesthesia study leave at Australia under Colombo plan for one year. In 1972, he was posted to Military Hospital. Cardiothoracic center, Pune (now called Army Institute of Cardiovascular and thoracic Sciences) and continued till he attained the rank as Air Cmdr. He distinguished to Command the Air Force Hospital Bangalore from 1981 – 1985 as Air Cmdr. and Air Vice Marshal. He came to AHRR, Deputy DGAFMS and finally DGMS (Air) at Delhi from 1986 – 1988. Post – retirement he was Consultant anesthesia at Sir Ganga Ram hospital where he worked for six years. He was married to Meera Bhalla, had two sons, elder one Dr. Neeraj Bhalla, a well - known cardiologist and the younger one an engineer Air Marshal Surender Kumar Bhalla suffered laryngeal carcinoma died at the age of 75 years.

- Air Marshal SK Bhalla was the first Air Force medical officer to achieve the rank as Air Marshal to become DGMS (Air).

- He was the first one to do Diploma and post – graduation (MD from Delhi University, anaesthesiology Armed Forces Medical services, without grading examination at AFMC Pune. Then he was posted to AFMC Pune to train other medical officers as anesthesiologists.

- He was confidence of the surgeons to operate critical war trauma patients – the exemplary trend to set in the speciality of anesthesiology.

- He was elected President of Research society of anaesthesiology – clinical pharmacology, 1986.

- Indian Military Medicine will always remember his contribution to critical care anesthesiology, shock management, care of sick and wounded during crisis of war 1962 and high – altitude disease.

- His family has instituted Air Marshal SK Bhalla Gold Medal at AFMC to be awarded annually to the person standing first in MD anesthesia.

Air Marshal Bhalla is settled at J – 159, Sector 25, Noida 201301 (Mob. 9213560926) inputs from Dr. Neeraj Bhalla, Delhi.

Air Marshal Surender Kumar Bhalla was post-graduate teacher and guide to Brigadier (Dr) Yudhvir Suri, VSM author of this book at Pune University, AFMC Pune 1972-1974 for Doctorate in Medicine Anaesthesiology (MD Anaesthesiology).

Military Surgeon: Lieutenant General

Bijoy Nandan Shahi: Army Medical Corps

(Physician – Cardiologist)

Armed Forces Medical Services: India

Lieutenant General Bijoy Nandan Shahi, Padma Bhushan, PVSM, AVSM, VSM was born on 18th January, 1942 at Samstipur (Bihar). His father was Zamindar freedom fighter and mother was a homemaker. He attended initial education, Khrist Raja High School, matriculation, Bettiah, Bihar and intermediate science, at LS College, Muzaffarpur (Bihar). He achieved high rank both in matriculation as well as in intermediate science. He then secured admission to prestigious Medical College Bihar University, Patna in 1959 and graduated in medicine MBBS with honors and distinction in 1964. He is a recipient of several academic awards during the graduation medical college period.

Lieutenant General Bijoy Nandan Shahi, was commissioned into the Army Medical Corps (AMC) on 15th August, 1964 and superannuated on 01st February, 2004 as Director – General Armed

Forces Medical Services (DGAFMS) India with distinguished 39 years and 3 months service.

He served as Medical Officer at Military Hospital Jabalpur and 423 Medical Bn. Then he was selected to the medical speciality of his choice, medicine, advance course, grading and Doctorate in Medicine (MD) AFMC Pune University in 1973. He served as clinical tutor at AFMC in department of medicine.

Lieutenant General Shahi served all commands and spent time as a medical specialist at IMTRAT Bhutan. Eastern command, he was posted at 155 Base Hospital Tezpur (Assam), 158 GH Bagdogra Siliguri, Military Hospital Danapur and Command Hospital (EC) Calcutta. He served Command Hospital (NC) Udhampur and Command Hospital (WC) Chandigarh.

General Shahi served the soldiers during war and peace at various Military Hospitals and simultaneously participated in educational forums in the Civil teaching medical institutes.

He delivered guest lectures, chaired scientific sessions and published research medical scientific papers in national and internation Journals. As a result he exceled a recognized personality in the field of medicine, precisely, the military medicine.

Lieutenant General Bijoy Nandan Shahi, further opted to the field of Cardiology. He did Post – doctorate in Cardiology (DM – Cardiology) from prestigious Post – graduate Institute of Medical Education and Research, Chandigarh India in 1981. He was awarded Fellowship American College of Cardiology 1997 and Academy of Medical Science (FAMS) 1998.

Lieutenant General Shahi served as Cardiologist in the capacity as Senior Advisor, consultant and Senior Consultant as Colonel, Brigadier and Major General at Armed Forces Clinic (1994 – 1997) and Army Hospital Research and Referral, New Delhi and Pune Universities to guide and train post graduates in medicine and cardiology. He had the distinction as Director, Principal and Commandant Army Hospital, Research and Referral, New Delhi.

He promoted the field of Cardiology beyond the boundaries of Army Hospital to the Zonal Hospitals of Armed Forces Medical Services. He became an architect of modern Cardiology with excellent infrastructure that delivered to the soldier.

Lieutenant General Shahi, became Director – General Hospital services at Medical Directorate, Ministry of Defence, India in 2009. It was the pride to serve professionalism in medicine, Armed Forces Medical Services from the level of senior advisor to Director – General Hospital services, AHQs New Delhi. It was further excellence to head the highest administrative positions Director – General Medical Services Army (2002 – 2003) and Director General Armed Forces Medical Services, Ministry of Defence Govt. of India (2003 – 2004)

Reaching the highest administrative positions, General Shahi, never compromised his clinical delivery to the soldier.

He continued to attend the patients during his busy schedules of appointments at the administrative levels.

Lieutenant General Shahi had the distinction of Padma Bhushan by President of India in 2004. He was Honorary physician to President of India in 2002 – 2004. He was awarded Rashtriya Ratana another significant civil award to his credit.

It was a unique honour, first time in the history of Indian Military Medicine, that, Lieutenant General Bijoy Nandan Shahi, was appointed Emeritus Medical Scientist (Cardiology) and Honorary Professor of Cardiology, Ministry of Defence and Armed Forces Medical College Pune. He held this position and continued working at Army Hospital, Research and Referral, New Delhi after his superannuation (2004 – 2008).

Lieutenant General Shahi is married, wife housemaker, elder son Dr. Madhkar Shahi, an eminent interventional Cardiologist, younger son Pushkar Shahi is B Tech (IIT Roorkee) and daughter Smitha is

Human & Finance management expert. General Shahi is settled at Gurugram (Haryana) Mob. 9910726012.

Indian Military Medicine will remember Lieutenant General Bijoy Nandan Shahi, Padma Bhushan, PVSM, AVSM, VSM as the architect of modern Cardiology and Medicine to Armed Forces India. He delivered the medicine to soldiers.

- *Honour and Award*

  Padma Bhushan
  He is only Army Medical Corps officer awarded this honour by President of India (2004)

  The other two officers have received Padma Shri Award.

Brigadier Radhakrishnan Sundara Rajan, VSM Military Surgeon: Cardiothoracic and Vascular Surgery Armed Forces Medical Services, India.

Born on 7th August 1942 at Pune. His father Late Shri Radhakrishnan was an engineer in Military Engineering Service and mother Late Jayalakshmi was housewife. Originally belonged to the state of Tamil Nadu. He had initial education at Tambaram and Tiruchirapalli, secured high position at interscience and enrolled to the prestigious Medical College Bangalore to complete graduation in 1964. (MBBS) During the medical college days, he had passion for surgery to achieve first position in the final. He was a keen sportsman and family background of military culture, he opted to join the army. He was commission in Army Medical Corps on 10th August 1964. Soon after passing MBBS, he join the Army, internship at MH Namkum and MOBC at AMC Centre South, Hyderabad. As a young medical officer he served the North-Western forward field area at Ladakh high-altitude regimental medical officer of the artillery battalion 66 field regiment officer incharge of advance dressing station of the medical battalion (ADS). He was granted advance surgery at Armed Forces Medical College, Pune 1968 to 1970, became a graded surgeon and simultaneously attained masters degree (MS) in surgery from Pune University in 1970. He was awarded Phadke prize by Pune University. He gained significant experience as an independent MO Surgeon in the field Ladakh Jammu and Kashmir, later General Surgeon 317 field hospital (1971-1974) at Sikkim military hospital Devlali (1974-1975) that was a significant contribution of medical delivery, precisely surgery to the soldier in peace and war.

1975, Brigadier Rajan, was posted to military hospital cardiothoracic centre (presently called Army Institute of Cardiothoracic and Vascular Sciences) as a general surgeon. He excelled in the chosen field, cardiothoracic surgery, did MCh in 1979 at Armed Forces Medical College, Pune University. His intense desire to adopt the latest and best surgical techniques ensured that the standard of his work was consistently world class. He did not stop to achieve further, secured Greenland Hospital fellowship (Auckland, New Zealand) under Sir Brian Barratt Boyes, 1979-1981. He returned to cardiothoracic centre Pune, improved several techniques, protocols and procedures as the modern standards of cardiothoracic surgery. Years later, in 1994, first coronary artery bypass surgery was done by him, started the CABG programme in Armed Forces Medical Services, India.

Brigadier Rajan retired from Armed Forces Medical Services, with distinction of Command Base hospital Delhi Cantt and consultant surgery, Command hospital, central command, Lucknow on 29th May 1999. Over the course of his career Brigadier Rajan, won several accolades such as lifetime achievement award, best alumni award of Bangalore Medical College, prestigious Vishist Seva Medal (VSM) by president of India. He published several research papers in national and international journal. He was executive committee member of Indian Association of Cardiothoracic surgery for several years, organised national conference at Pune and later became President in 1995, pride and honour, first time to an army cardiothoracic surgeon in India. He was dedicated teacher of MCh, MS, MBBS and BSc nursing students. After superannuation from army he was chief medical officer at Tata Tea hospital of Munnar (Assam) and spent time to voluntary work in community health. He is consultant with symbiosis health care (Education) Pune. He is married to Mrs. Kuttyamma, blessed with two daughters Dr. Veena and Dr. Viji, both medical professional of repute.

- Brigadier Rajan had love for classical music, Carnatic and Hindustani. He was fond of reading non-fiction history. He was keen sportsman with interest of horse-riding, swimming, cycling, trekking and gliding. Indian Military Medicine find him a unique multidimensional personality. Presently settled at Pune. Contact no.: 09900496414

- Indian military medicine will remember Brigadier R S Rajan, VSM as the pioneer cardiothoracic surgeon to initiate modern techniques and procedures of cardiac surgery and coronary artery bypass surgery programme in Armed Forces Medical Services, India.

He will always be cherished as the dedicated teacher and those who attained further advanced the speciality to the level of cardiac transplant in the ArmedForces Medical Services, India.

Lieutenant General Manoj Luthra

Military Surgeon: Cardiothoracic and Vascular Surgery Armed Forces Medical Services, India

Born 24 June 1957 at Delhi. His father Late Brigadier H R Luthra was a general surgeon in army medical corps and mother Late Smt Naj Luthra was housewife. His native place was Delhi. He had initial education at Mount Saint Mary's School Delhi and Pre-medical at DAV College Jalandhar (Punjab). He secured admission to his choice to become a doctor in the army at Armed Forces Medical College Pune in July 1972 to complete medical graduation in 1976. He was commissioned to Army Medical Corps, Armed Forces Medical Services on 27 February 1977. Since he was from AFMC, Pune, soon after, passing MBBS he joined the army, did his internship and MOBC to become the military medical officer. As a young medical officer he served field area Jammu and Kashmir, Rajouri-Poonch, 1978-1980. He was regimental medical officer, to prestigious Madras Regimental Centre, Wellington (Tamil Nadu). He was selected for advance course surgery at Armed Forces Medical College, Pune to attain "graded specialist" and master's post graduation (MS) under the doyen medical leadership of Lieutenant General

H S Puri, professor of surgery, AFMC Pune, 1983. He gained significant expertise as a general surgeon at military hospital, Gwalior (1986-1988) and other medical facilities Armed forces. Thereafter he was posted at Armed Forces Medical College, Pune as a lecturer faculty in general surgery. He had passion to master the expertise, innovate new techniques and critical care in war surgery, therefore, opted for the diligous critical care cardiac surgery training at Cardiothoracic Centre, AFMC, Pune. He qualified MCh under the excellent guide and teacher, Brigadier Radhakrishnan Sundara Rajan, CTC-AFMC, Pune University. He underwent further training in coronary artery bypass surgery at Royal Prince Alfred Hospital, Sydney, Australia (1990-1991). His passion and area of special interest is paediatric neonatal cardiac surgery in complex congenital diseases of the heart. He mastered the skills, art of surgery, as a senior registrar in cardiac surgery in the NHS, United Kingdom, 1991-93. He further secured fellowship in cardiac transplantation from Cleveland Heart Clinic, USA (2002). Lieutenant General Luthra is credited 15000 cardiac surgeries that includes 8000 Coronary artery bypass surgeries, 3 cardiac transplantations, aneurysmal repairs and complex congenital neonatal surgeries. He has been an academician par excellence, MCh examiner, guide and teacher at various universities. He is author of the widely read book "Paediatric Cardiac Intensive Care", research papers in national and international indexed journals. He is recipient of several awards, notably, Vishisht Seva Medal by President of India and professional medical societies in India. He has been professor and head, Cardiothoracic Centre, and Dean Armed Forces Medical College, Pune. He got superannuation 30 June, 2014 after distinguished 38 years of service. Post retirement he has been Director - CEO Jaypee Max Hospital, Noida - New Delhi NCR since 2014 till today.

- General Luthra is married to Dr. Neena Luthra, pathologist, medical professional, blessed with two daughters Mrs. Nidhi Luthra Bhatia, (IT professional) Ms. Nupur Luthra (content writer). Settled at Noida - New Delhi. Contact: 9711903241

Indian Military Medicine will remember Lieutenant General Manoj Luthra, VSM for his distinguished services of Cardiac surgery to the soldiers of Armed Forces Medical Services, India. He will be known as the founder of Paediatric cardiac surgery Armed Forces India. He will be contributor to excellence in military medicine to start the Cardiac transplantation in Armed Forces Medical Services, India.

Photograph by Indu Suri at Lal Villas, Hotel and Resorts, Nimrana – Behror NH – 8 Highway, Village Hamjapur 301701 (Rajasthan) June 2024

RURAL INDIA ECONOMY

Rural India economy is the credibility of Armed Forces: employability and infrastructure.

Indu Suri and Brigadier (Dr.) Yudhvir Suri, VSM invested their arrear credits from government of India, 2010, at Behror (Rajasthan) to facilitate the rural growth of India.

Photograph shows Mrs. Indu Suri with local folk lady in her traditional attire.

Couple Bird Spreads the message:

"Togetherness facilitates the recreation – regeneration, happiness to face new challenges"

– "Yudhvir Suri"

3

COMBAT STRESS & POST – TRAUMATIC STRESS DISORDER

SOLDIER – MILITARY MEDICINE

Soldier is itself an institution. Institution works as an army Constitution, spirituality and religion. Constitution is the discipline and lifestyle of the Soldier. Religion is his fighting spirit. All combined; discipline, lifestyle, religion and Spirituality promotes work, culture and finally facilitates. health. It is the health of the individual and community that leads to the health of the fighting Unit for victory in war.

Constitution of India is the supreme legal document of India. The document lays down the framework that demarcates fundamental, political code, structure, procedures, powers and duties of the government institutions and sets out fundamental rights, directive principles and the duties of the citizens. It was adopted by the Constituent Assembly of India on 26th November 1949 and became effective on 26th January 1950.

Armed Forces India adopted the Constitution of India as fundamental governing document that became the Republic of India.

The Army Act, 1950 is an act of parliament that governs military law in the Indian Armed forces. It was passed by the Parliament on May 22, 1950 and came into effect on July 22, 1950. The title is "An act to consolidate and amend the law relating to the government of the regular Army."

Armed Forces India adopted "The Army Act 1950," to govern the discipline and administration of the Armed Forces. Army Act 1950 laid certain restrictions on the soldier as the citizen of India. Thus, the soldier's constitution is discipline, life style and religion as enshrined in the Constitution of India.

Military medicine is all about Soldier, health and disease during peace and war, the men directly or indirectly Connected in caring the Wounded in the combat zone. Destructive weapons and military medicine developed parallel to each other. All those who care the wounded in war are called the "Military Surgeons" irrespective of their field of specialty, in language of military medicine. Innovation is the art of intelligence, that is, essentially integrated and applied to the sick and wounded. Clinical acumen, more than, the medical gadgets will be needed in the forward lethal operational Zone to save critically injured. Sanitation neglect or non-compliance of community medicine may cause defeat due to disease rather than the weapons of the enemy

Military Commanders need to have the strategy to care the wounded during battle. Military Medical investment benefits the soldier in long-terms.

- *Brigadier Yudhvir Suri, Indian Military Medicine, Volume 2, ISBN 978 – 93 - 5896 – 048 - 8 (é' book) 978 – 93 – 5896 -471 - 4 (Hard Cover) Zorba books Pvt. Ltd., Gurugram, April 2024.*

- *Brigadier Yudhvir Suri, Indian Military Medicine, Super – high altitude medical impact on soldiers. ISBN 978 – 93 – 5896 – 003 - 7 (Print book) 978 – 93 – 5896 – 004 - 4 (E-book) Zorba books Pvt. Ltd, Gurugram, 2023.*

- *Austin Granille, The Indian Constitution, Corner stone of a Nation, Oxford University Press ISBN 978 – 01 – 9564 – 959 - 8, year 1999*

- *Brigadier Karan Rathore (Retd) Failure of Indian Military Leadership in 1962 Sino-Indian Conflict: A re - look Swarajya magazine (defence) November 2024*

SPIRITUALITY, STRESS AND HEALTH:

Stress, spirituality, religion and health are inter-related to mitigate psychological, emotional, mental and physical well-being. Religious, stress coping framework facilitates social and emotional support hope and optimism, perception of control of self, behavioral change and decreases fear and insecurity. It works on the concept of faith-based asset of the believer. Individual adjusts assessment of situation, looks for an opportunity rather than a threat. He utilizes the Coping resources to turn down the situation as stressful. Daily perceived stress is managed with daily day-in day-out religious rituals. Frequency of prayers is often an indicator of greater stress. Religious people experience the more stress, rely more on religious coping resources, Personal faith may be considered as an adjustment to predict positive stressful situation and positive well-being through, transition. Prayers lo personal deity rituals may be beneficial on well-being.

One mechanism for dealing with pernicious effects of stress is faith- spiritual belief system. It protects the individual during adversity or crisis. Spiritual resources work at daily level, that is, how do individuals use their daily rituals and belief to attenuate the effects of stress on negativity spirituality is the inherent part of faith, similar to, religious coping resources.

Religious coping regulate the effects of stress on negativity and life style medical disorders (Hyper- tension, diabetes, and metabolic dysfunctions). Spirituality decreases the risk factors of well-being. It significantly controls the glycemic levels. Religious identity, race and gender work in favour of positive well-being. Increased participation with religious coping resources has been documented to decrease the cholesterol, healthier waist-hip ratio and allostatic load. Positive religious coping buffers the weight gain, emotional distress and the metabolic Control as the indicators of stress.

- *Allostatic: physiological process that helps organisor adjust to environmental demands by anticipating and regulating their energy use.*

- *Whitehead, B R Bergeman, CS Daily religious coping buffers the stress - affect relationship and benefit overall metabolic health in older adults. Psychology Relig spiritual, 14, (4) 12, 393-399, 2019 University of Michiga - Dearborn and University of Notre Dame*

- *Koenig HG; Research on Religion spirituality and mental health. A review Can J psychiatry 54, 283 - 291, 2009.*

- *McEwen B; Stellar E; stress and the individual mechanisms leading to disease. archives of Interval medicine, 153, (18) 2093 - 2101, 1993.*

- *The term "Allostatic load" the wear and tear on the body which accumulates as an individual exposed to repeated chronic stress, was coined by Mc Éwen and stellar in 1993. Chronic stress of neural or neuroendocrine response is the cause of physiological -disturbances-exhaustion, overload breakdown.*

Religion coping skills deal with the perceived stress or strains of daily life. It works on the concept:

- Self confidence that all acknowledge to the personal God or deity

- Defers - God will do! passively attributes responsibility to God..

- Involves partnership between. God and individual for positive adjustment.

High spiritual well-being scale is associated with low incidence of depression, schizophrenia, psychosis, negative emotions, conflicts and mental disorders. 1983, WHO East - Mediterranean countries proposed spiritual health in the draft resolution in

addition to physical, mental and social health. Health for all, strategies a spiritual dimension as defined in that resolution.

- *World Health Organisation Publication Issue 92902/1407 chapter 4. The spiritual dimension 1991*

- *Koenig HG; Religion spirituality and health. The research and clinical implications: ISRN psychiatry, 2012, 27, 87, 30.*

- *Ellison CG; Levin JS; The religion, health Connection. Evidence, theory, and future dimensions. Health education and behavior. 25 (6) 700 - 720, 1998.*

- *Seybold K; Hill Pc; The Role of religion and spirituality in mental and physical health. Curr directions in psychological science. 10(1) 21 - 24, 2001*

- *Seeman T; Dubin LF, Seeman M. Religiosity spirituality and health. A clinical review of the evidence for biological pathways. American psychologist 58 (1) 53 - 63, 2003*

- *Bradshaw matt et al Perceptions of accountability to God and psychological well-being among us adults. J. of Religion and health. 61(1) 327 - 352, 2022.*

Religious-spiritual factors related to health outcomes. Believrs who work towards the religious events or services are known to have low mortality rate. They have positive attribution to lifestyle. There is low incidence of alcoholism, cardiovascular disease and improved immunity system. They lack mood changes, irritability, irrationality and gain physical health. Those who attend the religious places have been found to be associated with high life-expectancy as a result of social group activities that benefits the healthy outcome. Low risk factors, result in lower incidence of illness, morbidity and mortality. However, negative impact of the religion has also been reported the literature. Elderly, sometimes, believe that God is punishing them as a result of isolation or illness. Negativity impact causes mortality. Guruji and many saints of modern world have recommended the devotees to remain in-door, perform prayers and rituals within the domestic environment. It facilitates the infirm, handicap and elderly.

Religious rituals; Hinduism, Islam and Christianity is known to increase the infection in the community as a result of practices or over-crowding. Prayer for someone sick or in crisis may be controversial. It may have positive effect on the health for whom prayed or fail to produce significant effects. However, intercessory prayers create community support to the individual that may impact psychological positive health.

Religiousity has been found to mitigate the negative impact of income inequality and injustice on health satisfaction. Believers experience higher status, dignity, and self-esteem. People religious or spiritual have better mental health adopt better to adverse situations and illness. Religion offers security, value of life, human relationship as a result of group activities and social support. These are the indicators of good health.

Negativity is pre-curse to psychological, Emotional, Mental and Physical medical disorder. Stress deteriorates it further. Therefore, negativity and stress must be managed at early stage aggressively. Religion may be powerful purposeful tool for combating stress and negativity. It may offer community support as well. It attributes sense of peace and calm to reduce stress. Religious faith is blind trust with super power at work in the world, meditation, prayers, yoga, that, are the ways to reduce stress in crisis and life, further, to achieve good health.

- *Dinakar Peri; over half of army personnel under severe stress. The Hindu news, 8 January, 2021 (United service Institution of India (USI) think tank study)*

Prolonged exposure of Indian Army personnel to Counter Insurgency and Counter terrorism environment has been one of the contributory factors for increased stress. There has been substantially greater loss than operational casualties suffered by the Armed forces.

Soldiers have increased incidence of lifestyle disorders (hypertension, diabetes, heart ailments) mental diseases (psychosis and neurosis) and psychosomatic disorders" officers experience comparatively much higher cumulative stress level compared to Junior Commission Officers (JCO's) and Other Ranks (OR) Army Officer's causative stress may be as under: -

- Inadequacies in quality of leadership
- Overburdened Commitments.
- Inadequate resources
- Frequent dislocations.
- Lack of transparency and fairness in postings.
- Lack of promotion avenues
- Insufficient accommodation
- Indifferent attitude of civilian officials.

Among lower rank officials:

- ❖ Excessive engagements
- ❖ Domestic problems
- ❖ Lack of dignity
- ❖ Lack of recreational facilities.
- ❖ Conflict with seniors and Subordinates

Impact of stress on Combat:

- ❖ Increased indiscipline incidents in Units and Sub-Units.
- ❖ Unsatisfactory state of training.
- ❖ Inadequate equipment maintenance
- ❖ Low morale.
- ❖ Adverse Combat -preparedness and operational performance

Stress prevention and management was suggested to be treated "as a leadership role at unit and formation level."

Defence Institute of Psychological Research (DIPR) identified Leave as the factor causing suicides amongst the soldiers at field and peace, other, recommendations were as Under:

- Leave grant rationalisation.

- Counselling at the time of leave

- Education in tenure of deployment

- Decreased workload.

- Increase pay-allowances

- Improve living conditions.

- Better interpersonal relationship between officers and men.

- Stress management- training programmes.

- Recreational activities.

- Psychological Counselling

- Grievance redressal

MILITARY PSYCHIATRY

Army has denied severe stress among the soldiers of Armed Forces in India. Institutional counter-steps have been initiated from time to time with quality of facilities, psychological counselling, yoga, meditation, stress management training and military psychiatry. Advance military psychiatry centres have been established at INHS Asvini, Mumbai; Vishakhapatnam, Kochin, Port Blair, Goa and Karwar.

There may be denial but on ground soldiers suffer Stress and stress related disorders. It needs to revolutionalise the military psychiatry services in Indian Armed Forces Medical Services:

- Psychiatry Consultation. should be extended to soldiers - open system rather than the "closed - door Unit referral" system.

- Institutionalise the psychiatry nursing-qualified nurses. Rather than the male nursing assistants or ward-boys system of ancient world.

- Psychiatry management is no more a taboo to the soldier Awareness education needed."

- Forward psychiatry services to the soldier in the field, beyond the Zonal hospitals of the present day, including psychotherapy.

- Early psychiatry management in the forward field prevents the late sequelae, even the lifelong psychosomatic disorders.

The remedial measures at individual soldier level, institutional level and medical management level should be integrated and initiated to deliver to the soldier at the field and peace. Soldiers may claim disability of post – traumatic stress disorder from the state that may be years after their superannuation with record of their service in operational zone.

- *"Psychiatry Nursing" is a specialty of 2 years diploma after BSc nursing courses, of the qualified nurse.*

Stress Vs Exhaustion

Stress is beneficial. It promotes adaptability, stimulus to adrenaline secretion to overcome crisis, works to increase performance, productivity and revenue. It facilitates life-style. It promotes the cognitive-equity concept to create inclusive environment. Many people say they work better with good results under stress. Human body has inbuilt System to cope the phenomenon of stress called General Adaptation Syndrome (GAS). However, stress should never be stretched to the level of exhaustion, General Adaptation System fails, that deteriorates the body responses to adverse outcome. One needs to understand the level of stress to level of exhaustion.

Stress manifests as acute delayed or chronic in the form of physical, psychological and emotional disorder. Early manifestation may be exhaustion such as tiredness, burnout, loss of sleep, lethargy, quarrel – like mood, irritability and violence on menial issues. Early recognition and early remedial measures will prevent the long-term adverse effects on health.

- *Raju MSVK, Srivastva K, Chaudhury S, Saluja SK, quantification of stressful life events in service personal. Ind. J. psychiatry, 43, 213 – 218, 2001*

COMBAT STRESS

Combat stress is the military term related to the experiences of the soldiers such as fighting against the enemy at the forward area or counter insurgency, temporary duties (at short notice) promotions (rank structure), isolation and postings to super – high altitude. The word stress is derived from the Latin "Stringi" that means "To be drawn Tight." "Workforce" stress is the alternate term used in the civil. Some people describe stress as the competition, selection, challenges, workload, and time pressure. These are the stressors that may cause the reaction. These reactions may manifest as "strains" which can be physiological, behavioral, cognitive, psychosomatic, emotional and sometimes, non-specific responses of the body. In medicine Hans Selye proposed, GAS – general adaptation syndrome, as a stress response of the body, that explains reaction of the body under three stages: (1) Alarm stage (2) Resistance stage (3) Exhaustion stage. It says stress improves performance till an individually determined tolerance is reached when exhaustion sets in and impairs performance. Stress may be classified acute or chronic. Acute stress is sudden in onset, severe in degree, as seen in combat crisis situations. Chronic stress is slow insidious in onset, moderate in severity as seen in the service environment, denial of promotions or familial results of isolation. Whatever may be the reason or type of stress, it needs stress management at the individual level or community and organizational level. It does not help to avoid stress or postpone the expert management or intervention.

How to measure stress? There is no "Ready to read" measure scale system", like thermometer but needs to be worked with the individual on the cumulative score based on life change units or scaling of life events. It is the questionnaire – response that each response is allotted the number of points. Finally, all points are cumulated to be placed in the scale to determine the severity of stress. Life change unit system (Holmes and Rahe) and scaling of life events (Paykel) were western based. In India presumptive stressful life events (PSLES) have been developed but none were military or paramilitary use. Raju et al, 2001 quantified the stressful life events in service personals and named as the "AFMC life events" scale. The study is in agreement that soldering is stressful and evidence exists that stress consequences are seen on the Indian soldiers.

In India, psychiatry service, in Armed Forces Medical services, is only in large peace based zonal hospitals, therefore, it does not reflect the true level of combat stress in the Indian soldiers. No such study is available amongst the soldiers at the field forward operational zones. Soldiers suffered the horrors of war during World War 1 at the frontline. Many of those veterans returned home with memories of suffering that they had witnessed, that was called "SHELL SHOCK" later known as post traumatic stress disorder (PTSD) syndrome.

1915, British army in France was instructed "Shell-shock" casualty to have prefixed "W" if it were due to the enemy and wear a wound stripe (wound medal). In case the individual breakdown was not due to the enemy explosion it was labelled shell-shock "S" that denoted sickness. Those who were prefixed "W" with wound medal were entitled to rank as wounded with pension while labelled "S" were treated as sickness.

Combat stress incidence varies between 15% - 25% depending upon the enemy contact and intensity of the fighting. All armies the world over, have admitted that their soldiers have suffered combat fatigue syndrome. The ratio of stress casualties to battle casualties may be as high 1: 1. It may be less with low intensity war 1: 10. World

War II, European Army rate of stress casualties was 1 in 10 (101 : 1000) troops per year. Counter-insurgency also reported stress fatigue amongst the soldiers but less than the continuous combat operations of modern warfare.

Combat fatigue is well defined disease entity as acute stress reaction, that may pre-curse to post-traumatic stress disorder. In military medicine it is difficult to miss the manifestation of the soldier as typically called "thousand-yard stare" an unfocused, despondent weary gaze, to diagnosis of combat fatigue. (See title page)

Fatigue related cognitive dysfunctions progress to serious threat to life such as

- Anxiety, irritability, depression

- Substance abuse

- Disruptive behavior

- Loss of adaptability

- Mistrust of others

- Confusion

- Suicidal tendencies

- Loss of self-control

Combat stress is recognized with the symptoms:

◈ Irritability and anger outbursts

◈ Excessive fear and worry

◈ Aches pains all over the body

◈ Exhaustion - fatigue

◈ Depression and apathy

◈ Loss of sleep or sleep disturbance

◈ Loss of appetite

◈ Personality changes to invoke non-visible, non-perceptible super natural power

◈ Change of behavior- submissive or violent

Combat stress is usually temporary, sometimes, natural reaction, experienced by the soldier to the traumatic crisis. It disappears with rotational leave policy of the organization. Post traumatic stress disorder syndrome is more severe that lasts > 1 month and persists for months and years even after the individual is removed from the acute crisis situation.

World War 1 is reported to have 57% soldiers who became casualties either killed or wounded. Combat stress was applied to the stress reaction in the military environment. Soldier's mental breakdown was considered a psychiatric illness, later it was labelled as shell-shock disease.

World War II, it was the prolonged posting of the soldiers, fighting on the forward frontline, intensity and frequency of the combat that evolved the cause of the soldier to suffer. The term that was used in World War 1 and even earlier as Nostalgia, psychiatric disorder, shell-shock became known as combat fatigue or operational exhaustion in the World War II

- *Selye H; stress and psychiatry American J psychiatry, 111, 276, 1956*

- *Holmes TH; Rahe RH; the social readjustment rating scale, J psychosomatic Research, 11, 213 – 218, 1967.*

- *Paykel E S; scaling of life events, Arch Gen psychiatry, 25, 340 – 347, 1971*

- *Singh G, Kaur D; Kaur H; presumptive stressful live events scale for use in India. Ind. J. psychiatry 26, 107 – 114, 1984.*

- *Saldanha D, Goel DS, Kapoor S, Garg A, Kochar HK, posttraumatic stress disorder in polytrauma. Med J Armed Forces, India, 49, 7 -10, 1996*

- *Puri SK, Sharma PC, Naik CRK, Banerjee A, Ecology of combat fatigue among troops engaged in counter-insurgency operations. Med J Armed Forces India, 55, 315 – 318, 1999*

Failure of general adaptation syndrome (GAS) as a result of fight or flight, dampens the sympathetic stimulator response and return to homeostasis. During this period of resistance physical and mental activity may be reduced. Long combat involvement depletes the body resources to render it dysfunctional and that causes the exhaustion. Multiorgan dysfunction may be seen when the body remains in a state of stress, sometimes, extended exhaustion can permanently damage the body.

- *Hans Selye, stress and the general adaptation syndrome Brit Medical Journal 1 (4667) 1383 – 1392, 1950*

- *Plessct MR, Psychoneurotics in combat. Am. J. Psychiatry, 103, 87 – 88, 1946*

- *G Fontenot, Fear God and Dreadnaught: Prepare a unit for confronting Fear, Military review (July – August) 13 – 24, 1995*

POST-TRAUMATIC STRESS DISORDER

Military service is the most common cause of posttraumatic stress disorder (PSID). Those who were deployed at hostilities and participated in the combat operations, had the risk of developing PTSD. Earlier it was the trauma life-threat experience of military called as shell-shock but later deliberated to the concept of balance needs stress management at the individual community and environmental level.

Posttraumatic stress disorder may develop after a gap of months or even years that the soldier had experienced. It is the recurrent intrusive reminders of the traumic life-event that flashes as the nightmare. The acute stress reaction penetrates as the slow panic attack and persists life-time disorder. Negative thoughts and mood, belief of self and surrounding world becomes persistent fear, and guilt. It becomes difficult to articulate the positive emotions. Bad memories cause withdrawal from friends, family and environment. Hyperalert results emotional reactivity, irritability, anger and violence.

Early symptoms of PTSD

- ◈ Intrusive thoughts ….. recurrent.

- ◈ Nightmares – vivid disturbing dreams.

- ◈ Memory loss

- ◈ Negative thoughts about self and environment world

- ◈ Self - isolation, apathy

- ◈ Anxiety, irritability, anger

- ◈ Loss of interest in favourite activities

- ◈ Panic reaction

Traumatic life – events impact the brain functioning. Hippocampus, amygdala, and prefrontal cortex are strongly associated with stress and memory. When something traumatic happens, memory loss results as natural defensive mechanism. These unpleasant memories resurface, time and time again, therefore, it is a cause of distress.

Stress disorder has been documented as early as 630BC. PTSD has been termed as soldiers heart during civil war 1861 – 1865, shell shock in World War 1, combat fatigue during World War II, Vietnam syndrome after the Vietnam war. 6% of civil population was documented with traumatic event experience. 11–25% of soldiers who served in Iraq, operation Iraqi freedom and Afghanistan, operation Enduring freedom have reported PTSD.

Ancient military medicine documented the condition by Hippocrates, holy book of bible, The Epic of Gilgamesh, described soldiers who experienced intrusive memories and nightmares about the war. These experiences of the soldiers depict the present-day PTSD.

Dr. Johannes Hofer, Swiss physician, used the term "nostalgia" amongst the Swiss military soldiers, Hermann Oppenheim, a Germen doctor called "traumatic neurosis" to describe the condition that arose in the survivors as a result of railway accidents in early 1800s. Honigman (1907) a German psychiatrist coined the term "war neurosis"

During World War 1, 1914 -1915, Soldiers of British Expeditionary. Force, experienced tinnitus, amnesia, dizziness, tremors, headache, , hyper - sensitivity to noise after the combat. The condition resembled of the physical head injury but there were no signs of head wounds. British officers and enlisted men were experiencing nervous mental shock. Charles Myers (1915) was the first to document in lancet coined term. "Shell-shock" during the Battle of loos World War 1. It was the earliest description of the condition linked to the artillery shell explosion. However, many soldiers experienced PTSD but did not expose to artillery fire or proximity to exploding shell. Nor did the shell – shock resulted from the poisoning by carbon monoxide as a result of artillery explosion. There was alternate debate describing shell – shock as emotional rather than the physical trauma.

Military leadership failed to recognize "Shell – shock" a medical disorder. It was considered a weakness, discipline disorder, military crime of desertion and cowardiceness. Many were put on trial and executed.

- Jones E; Fear NJ; Wessely S; shell shock and mild traumatic brain injury – a historical review. The Am. J psychiatry 164 (11) 1641 – 1645, 2007

- Myers CS; A contribution to the study of shell – shock. Lancet (1) 316 – 320, 1915.

- Macleod AD; shell shock – Gordon Holmes and the great War. J. of royal society of medicine 97 (2) 86 – 89, 2004

- US advance research agency has reported the blast affects on the brain. It revealed that brain remains intact after low levels of blast effects but the blast initiates chronic inflammation afterwards that results shell – shock syndrome and PTSD.

- Preventing violent explosive neurologic trauma (Peavent) www.darpa.mil (2019)

Concussion theory of microscopic brain lesions was argued as the cause of "Emotional Stressor" of post – traumatic stress disorder. It evolved the concept of physio neurosis – somatic psycho – physiology as the cause of PTSD. Men under stress became the reflection of psychiatry. **During World War II, it was the initiation of combat psychiatry, a major contribution of the specialty in military medicine.**

Post traumatic stress disorder (PTSD) is a common mental health concern amongst the soldiers (10%) compared to the civil population (6.0%). World War II, sometimes, called "total war" targeted civil population, used artillery, tanks, nuclear missiles and weapons of mass – destruction that demoralized the civilians as well the military. It resulted PTSD in the military personnels. The risk factors were:

- Combat experience
- Deployment to a war zone without combat
- Combat casualty, trauma
- Witnessing death
- Prisoner of war or torture

These soldiers who suffered PTSD had significant impact on mental and physical health such as:

- Sucidal behavior
- Increased substance use
- Marital disturbances
- Lack of self - care and quality of life, disinterest.
- Impaired work performance or lack of concentration

- Self - isolation
- Nightmares, horror dreams,
- Negative thoughts of self and the world
- Intrusive thoughts - recurrence
- Anger, violence on minor issues of daily life
- Avoidance Events

- someone nearly drowned will avoid even taking bath because it reminds them the incidence of crisis.

- those experience the life event, would see the self and the world "foreshortened" future that is the negative world. To build the self – esteem, worthy of life and assurance may be a slow but success therapy.

- Vivid flash back

  Flash back is the feel as though the traumatic life event is happening all over again.

  It is different than the intrusive recurrent thoughts. This may result panic, with aggressive response. There may be trigger factors such as noise or subtle sound, light flicker and even shadow image.

  Those who faced vivid flash back are encouraged distraction, to ground themselves with five senses.

- Casting self - blame

  PTSD victims blame themselves after a traumatic life event particularly that resulted injury or death to others. Sometimes, assign blame to others associated with the accident.

- Alcoholism:

  The international society of Traumatic stress studies document 30% of those survived violent life events go on to alcoholism. It is the way to "drown out" the pain experienced from PTSD.

Indian soldiers manifest as psychosomatic or psychiatric disorders, 24.3% incidence of PTSD after polytrauma. Armed forces veterans are documented to have PTSD as under:

- Operationally deployed: 18.6%
- Non - operational deployed: 13.8%
- Airforce active deployed: 6.6%
- Airforce nonactive deployed: 6.2%
- Naval deployed veterans: 12.3%
- Naval nondeployed veterans: 10.1%

World War II, there was perplexity regarding the shell – shock stress disorder. Huge number of officers and enlisted soldiers were seen walking dazed and confused. They left their posts at the forward frontline. Replenishment, soldier shift was the problem at the frontline combat. Military medicine was not clear at the combat stress disorder syndrome nor the military leadership accepted the medical cause of the condition of the soldiers. They were accused of desertion, cowardice and malingering. Military leadership invoked the laws of military discipline, large number of military personnels were court martialed, large number were awarded death penalty and 346 British soldiers were shot on the orders of military command.

Combat is a French word, means "fight", that is a purposeful violent conflict between multiple combatants with the intent to harm the enemy. Combat may be armed or unarmed. Combat stress was recognized as the acute behavioral disorganization as a result of trauma of war. Combat fatigue, operational exhaustion or battle neurosis were the terms used from time to time that became the diagnosis of combat psychiatry.

Soldering is stressful, including those non-combatants (doctors, paramedics, nurses, civilians in defense services, and military logistic services) posted to the operational zones are

prone to stress consequences. Indian army incidence is not alarming but soldiers are not immune to combat as experiences from other Armed Forces in the world, UK, USA, Russia, Germany, France Soldiers encounter constant threat to life during counter – insurgency, inhospitable terrain, climate, uncongenial environmental that is bound to cause mental morbidity. Small trivial stress may deteriorate the depleted General Adaptation Syndrome (GAS) to adversely affect the safety of the soldier.

- *VSSR Ryali, Bhat PS, Srivastava, Kalpana, stress in Indian Armed Forces how true and what to do. Medical Journal Armed Forces India, 67 (3) 209 – 211, 2011 (edition)*

- *Kushwaha AS, stress in Armed Forces, how true and what to do. Medical Journal Armed Forces India 18, 68 (1) 90, 2012.*

Combat psychiatry is highlighted in Indian military medicine. It is stressed in military leadership that "sensitive and sensible" command reduces the tragic incidents and consequences.

Siachen, toughest of the soldiers may crumble under the stress of combat. Combat stress is inevitable part of the deployment of unconventional warfare. However military leadership needs to be alert on the issue of soldiers combat stress as duty bound to the men under command.

Perplexity of terminology or diagnosis does not mean to label the soldier as malingerer, administer the death warrant. Military medicine is the reflection of medicine in the civil. No such condition was documented in medicine, though, description similar to the symptoms of combat or trauma stress has been reported in ancient literature and war situations.

- *Ramayana, 2500 years ago, document demon Marich experience, post – traumatic stress disorder like syndrome – hyper – arousal, reliving trauma, and avoidance behavior after being killed by an arrow.*

Post – traumatic stress disorder was diagnosed after 120 years, first such description was given during American Civil War 1861 – 1865 amongst the soldiers. Later acute reactions to combat were distinguished from delayed reactions after combat in 1945. In between there have been numerous terms and finally American psychiatry association (APA)documented in diagnostic and statistical manual (DSM III) 1980 and DSM – V) 2013 as the diagnosis of post – trauma stress disorder syndrome.

- *Mare Antonie Crocq and Louise Crocq. From shell shock and war neurosis to PTSD, a history and psychotraumatology. Dialogues clin neurosciences, March 2 (1) 47 – 2000*

During World War 1, French psychiatrists treated these patients of shell – shock near the operational zone of war. Frontline psychiatric Unit hospitals admitted these patients to benefit the emotional support of the comrades and likely to return back to their Unit. The concept evolved was to treat within the hearing distance of the frontline guns. It worked on five principles:

1. Immediacy:

    Treating as early as possible

2. Proximity:

    Treating as near as the frontline as possible

3. Expectancy:

    Positive expectation of as early treatment with psychotherapy

4. Simplicity:

    Simple treatment rest, sleep and reassurance

5. Centrality:

    Organized flow of psychiatric casualties from forward to rear with medical management doctrine.

Frederick, an American psychiatrist, rediscovered, "shell – shock" forward frontline management of World War 1 during North African Campaign in World War II 1943. First time the term "exhaustion" for combat was used in psychiatric cases.

- *Salmon TW; care and treatment of mental diseases and war neuroses shell shock in the British Army. Mental Health Hygiene, 1, 509 – 547, 1917*

- *Grinker and Spiegel, men under stress, Philadelphia, Pa: Blakiston, 1945*

Post – traumatic stress disorder, has been documented amongst the soldiers exposed to the combat during Vietnam War, 1964 – 1973. Combat stress was reported 11.5 per 1000 per year who were managed at the forward frontline psychiatric units. 25% of the soldiers who participated in the war, had the prevalence of PTSD and needed psychotherapy on their return to home. Similarly, it is seen in Indochina and Algeria hostilities. No soldier can escape the vagaries of combat and combat stress is common even in low conflict warfare or counter – insurgency.

- *Belenky G contemporary studies in combat psychiatry. Westport, conn: Greenwood press, 4, 1987*

- *Crocq L; Crocq MA; Barrois C; et al low intensity combat psychiatry casualties In Pichot P, Berner P editors psychiatry, the state of the art, New York, NY Plenum press 6, 545 – 550, 1985.*

PTSD is well defined consensus diagnosis, specific syndrome, in individuals who experience major life events.

Forward combat psychiatry management prevents the delayed or chronic stress related disorders.

Forward psychiatric management units are recommended in the army to benefit the soldiers.

4

ANAESTHESIOLOGY NEWS AND DEVELOPMENT

ANAESTHESIOLOGISTS' STRESS

Brigadier Yudhvir Suri, VSM

MBBS (Srinagar-Kashmir), MD (AFMC Pune)

Phd (BJMC Pune University), Cardiothoracic Anaesthesia Fellow (AIIMS, New Delhi)

FIMSA (India)

Veteran Consultant Anaesthesiology (Armed Forces Medical Services, India)

Stress may be defined as an adaptive syndrome, challenge to change, may be physical, environmental, emotional or psychological. It is body response to pressure, demand, life-threat or injury. It is an attempt to survive in a hostile, unpredictable and insensitive world. It is a reaction to destability demands. Pressures originate extrinsically and intrinsically from work environment and family engagements to create situations of stress. Physiologically, the human body has an adaptive system to function. Situation deteriorates when the individual fails to cope with the demands that necessitate to respond.

This is in simple terms, there is no consensus universal acceptance of definition in modern medicine.

No one is immune to stress, status, ethnicity, caste, or gender. History of anesthesia has documented anesthesia demo failures, displeasure, chemical abuse, addiction, and suicide. Prime Minister of India, Indira Gandhi has been depicted as having the guilt stress syndrome in the movie "Emergency" by Kangana Ranaut as actor-director. Physicians, as a community, has high incidence of alcoholism, drug abuse, depression, suicide, and psychiatric hospitalization. Specialty of Anesthesiology is concerned of still higher rates of chemical abuse and suicide compared to the general physician population. Anesthesiology is rated as the stress oriented medicine. Excessive stress affects the moral integrity, physical well-being, emotional and psychological stability and ability to care the safety of the patients.

Stress remains unavoidable in modern world. General public, physicians and soldiers are exposed to the life-events to experience the stress disorders. Awareness, education, training, early detection, self-coping, comrade, expert help and management will prevent the long-term adverse outcome.

Ancient medicine, Heraclitus, Hippocrates, Epicurus have preferred that health was a balance of elements and disease as a result of disharmony of forces. Later Thomas Sydenham declared the concept of adaptive response to disease. Then in the 19th century Claude Bernard, French physiologist, documented dynamic physiological internal equilibrium as the principle of health. Another physiologist, Walter Cannon coined the term "homeostasis", to extend the emotional and physiological realm, to the concept of the "flight or fight" reactions. He advocated the adaptive response to stress that was linked to the release of catecholamines.

Hans Selye, a physician, is the father of pressure-related stress syndrome - popularised the term "stress" as an umbrella word that connected the pressures experienced by the people. He declared that the only freedom from stress is the death. He emphasized non-specific physiological adaptive responses to the demands, threats and pressures (stressors). He labelled the phenomenon of General Adaptation Syndrome, usually termed as GAS, in the philosophy of anaesthesia. He laid the foundation of stress as homeostatic vehicle for adaptation, a physiological mechanism deployed to maintain the integrity and viability of an individual.

His real genius work has been that he recognized the "Diseases of Adaptation", that is the responses to change and pressure, might cause the pathophysiology and disease. It is the stressful, intense, sometimes protracted situation that causes the stress disorder.

He also described that all situations of threat to homeostasis were not injurious and coined the term "eustress" to define mild, brief and controllable states of challenged homeostasis that could be beneficial and serve as a positive impetus for growth and development.

Therefore, stress is unavoidable, beneficial till to recognize the level of exhaustion that will determine the adverse effects. We need to understand the essence, to cope and early management.

Situations differ, sometimes, minor emotional reaction may trigger the offending situation, whereas, we might be able to handle major emergencies with no sense of experience to stress. In fact, one may feel emotionally or physically exhausted at the end of the event. Whatever, may be the cause or situation self-determination and self-admission will be needed to expert help and early management.

- Helliwell PJ; Suicide amongst anaesthetists-in training. Anaesthesia 1983, 30, 1097.

- Bruce DL, Bide KA, Linde Hw, et al, causes of death among anaesthesiologists, a 20 year survey Anaesthesiology, 1968, 29, 565-569.

- Selye H; The stress of life. New York McGraw-Hill Book Co; 1984.

ANAESTHESIOLOGY-OCCUPATIONAL STRESS:

Anaesthesia has become safe for the patients but more challenging to the anaesthesiologists. Safety of anaesthesia has expanded to the extremes of age and critically sick. Expectations and demands of good clinical outcome, even in high-risk circumstances has been recognised. Malpractice litigations have haunted the self-esteem of the anaesthesiologist to be prone to suicide.

- Brimingham PK, Ward RJ, A high-risk suicide group: the anaesthesiologist involved in litigation, Aus J psychiat. 1985, 142, 1225-1228.

Clinically, anaesthesia needs to plan even short procedure may be elective or emergency. The standard of care is constant vigilance focus of sustained critical care. Best of care, best of experienced hands, good environment with trained staff, the clinical outcome still remains unpredictable. Anaesthesiologist maintains a state of physiological arousal which by definition is called stress. He suffers stress from the time word "go". This stress phenomenon is measured with progressive increase in heart-rate, called, tachycardia during the anaesthetic critical care for elective surgery. Tachycardia peaks at intubation, the skill needed to maintain anaesthesia and adequate ventilation. Tachycardia is related to the urgency of intubation, magnitude and clinical experience of the operator, even sometimes, premature ventricular contractions of the heartbeat is seen. Tachycardia and hypertension were recorded to those who were teaching the procedure in the operation theatre. Premature ventricular contractions (PVCs) and even ST-depression were recorded in these teachers.

- Xiao Y, Mackenzie CF, Bernhard W, et al; The Lotus group: dynamics of stress during elective and emergency airway management. Anaesthesiology, 1996; 85(3A) A 957.

- Toung TJ, Donham RT, Rogers MC. effect of providing medical training on the stress of giving anaesthesia. Anaesthesiology, 1986; 65(3A) A473.

- Azar I, Sophie's, Leark. The cardiovascular response of anaesthesiologists during induction of anaesthesia. Anaesthesiology, 1985; 63(3A) A76.

ANAESTHESIOLOGY: AGE, GENDER AND WORKPLACE RELATED STRESS.

Anaesthetists manpower is usually grouped into four specific stress related factors:

1. Residents-Trainees , Age < 30 years

2. Young anaesthetists , Age 30-40 years

3. Mid-life anaesthetists, Age 40-60 years

4. Senior anaesthetists, Age > 60 years.

Residents-Training period is taxing physically, psychologically and intellectually. They have textbook knowledge but limited skills and expertise. They work on the responsibility of teachers. They rely on the expertise and behavior of instructors at the workplace. They face harsh working conditions:

- Responsibility with limited experience early training.

- Sleep deprivation

- Long working hours

- Physical fatigue.

- Lack of respect, status

- Insecurity of position

- Focus on mistakes, mal-occurrences, bad outcome, catastrophies.

- Negativism from seniors.

- Lack of infrastructure to residents comforts.

- Lack of accommodation

Young anaesthetists (Age 30-40 years) is the period of anxiety developed in response to the challenges of clinical anesthesia. It is a protective period of extended training with scientific knowledge but limited exposure to clinical anesthesia, experience and wisdom. They need to deal stress as:

- Maturity

- Accommodating behavior

- Confidence

- Interpersonal relationships

- Medical education-training debt expenditure

- Expenses from domestic and family

- Job stability

- Professionalism status in the academic society.

Mid-life anaesthetist are the period that one has achieved professional stability, experience and wisdom. One is connected to the new generation in growth and the seniors who have attained their inspirations. They have the stress factors as:

- Self settlement and spouses

- Change of permanent residential property

- Children growth and emergence adolescence

- Financial resource discrepancies

- Increased family demands

- Restructure personal and family life-style.

- Professional status function and relationship.

- Parental responsibilities.

Senior anaesthetists (Age > 60 years) is the class of community that has achieved wealth of clinical experience with wide range exposure in the speciality, skill, expertise and comfort. They have gained some sort of name and fame in the scientific and social framework of the speciality.

The stress factors in this group:

- Aging susceptibility: physical, intellectual and emotional fatigue.

- Inability to deal heavy workload - pressure demands.

- Sleep deprivation

- Emergency night calls

- ill-health disabilities.

- Graceful phase-down clinical practice to retirement.

- Difficult to match the current knowledge, innovations and technical advances to new peri-operative medicine.

    ▲ Seeley HF The practice of anaesthesia - a stressor for the middle-aged? Anaesthesia 1996, 51, 571-574.

    ▲ McNamee R, keen RI, Corkill cm, Morbidity and Early retirement among anaesthetists and other specialists. Anaesthesia, 1987, 42, 133-140

Female anaesthetists have gender specific stress factors: The present-world is no longer male-dominant society. They have individual personal identity, choice and aspirations in the civil society.

- Discrimination with 'glass-ceiling' of remunerations and career

- Sexual harassment

- Unfavourable workplace environment.

- Pregnancy

- Child rearing and home-keeping.

- Primary care-taker during illness of parents, in-laws, husband and children.

- "Sandwitch generation" - eldercare with rearing children.

- Lack of personal care - physical and emotional stress causes anger, guilt and sense of loss

- Competition at workplace to outperform male colleagues to be treated equal and advance performer.

Academics: those in academics, teachers, research. have dual responsibilities: Training and clinical. They face production pressure for publication of research in the reputed medical journals that is mandatory to their career growth. They need to complete their clinical work-load of daily schedules. Inexperience in academics in the beginning of their career is stressful.

- Teaching is undervalued to clinical experience and acumen in professional growth.

- Research funds constraints is stressful to progress in academics, sometimes create conflict of interest and ethical dilemmas.

Rural Anaesthetists. Those in rural practice face the difficulties such as:

- Single anaesthetist in the community. No backup support in need of emergencies.

- Lack of call and vacation coverage

- Lack of professional relationship in the professional society.

- Lack of educational opportunities.

- Failure to update to the new advancements in the professional knowledge and skills.

- Limited revenue with limited workload.

  - ▲ McCall TB, The impact of long working hours on resident physicians. N Engl J Med, 1988, 318, 775-778.

▲ Katz JD, Factors leading to retirement among anaesthesiologists. Anaesthesiology 1997; (87- 3A) A1013.

Workplace:

◈ Operational design and structure is specific to anaesthesia work environment stress. It involves interaction relationship of anaesthetists with perioperative surgical and critical care teams, free flow from operating rooms to pre and post operative areas.

◈ Perioperative care is a dynamic collective responsibilities of personalities, competencies, cooperative spirit, motivation, work ethics, personal comforts with clearly defined boundaries. Operation theatre complex needs non-conflict specific function culture for optimal production.

◈ Noise is stressful to anaesthesia work environment.

- Monitors and alarms
- Suction apparatus
- Surgical machinery
- Electrocautery
- Ventilators
- Telephone-intercom
- Loud conversations

◈ Other factors:

- Exhaled vapours and surgical exhaust.
- Radiation
- Latex and infection exposures.
- Visual challenges - lasers, darkness, lighting, monitors.
- Uncomfortable furniture - working stations, chairs.

Auditory neural pathways are connected with the ascending reticular formation activating system and the diffuse thalamic projection systems involved in arousal and attention, hence, it is stressful. Noise cause sympatho-adrenal discharge in normal individuals, causes higher response in those with chronic anxiety or hypertension. Operation room noise can produce sympathetic nervous system hyperactivity. Noise can impair cognitive and psychological functions. It disturbs the verbal communication, short-term memory, information processing and mental efficiency. Interferes task management, induces annoyance and irritability."

- Shapiro RA, Berland T, Noise in the operating room. N Engl J Med, 1972, 287, 1236-1238.

- Murphy VS, Malhotra SK, Bala I, Raghunathan MD, Mental effects of noise on anaesthetists can J anaesth, 42, 608-811.

- Weinger MR, Englund CE, Ergonomic and human factors affecting anaesthetic vigilance and monitoring performance in the operating room environment. Anaesthesiology, 1990; 995-1021.

Music: has been a remedy in medicine, thought to possess the healing properties, ability to strengthen the intellectual capacity and enhance the creative spirit. Music has added to the modern design of the operation theatre to benefit the operating teams."

- Music is desirable as specific

  ▲ Selection – instrumental

  ▲ Timing to phases of surgery

  ▲ Auditory volume limits

- Weinger M, Cardiovascular reactivity among surgeons music to everyone's ears. JAMA 1995, 273, 1090.

Production pressures have become the norms of the economic and social demands of the workplace. Many places have focused

"Maximum number - minimum anaesthetising time", no interim case time delays, no cancellations, no postponements. It will be one of the stress factor to the anaesthesiologist causing:

- decision-making case management

- Conditioned production pressure behaviour

- Controlling cost vs safety

- Potentially unsafe delivery culture

- Ethically and morally unacceptable.

- Damaging to self-esteem

Production efficiency should not be at the cost of patient safety.

Workplace stressors:

- ◈ Unpredictable, uncontrollable long work hours.

- ◈ Erratic opportunities for meals, and nutrition.

- ◈ Hydration (Tea-breaks)

- ◈ Washroom breaks

- ◈ Isolation for long hours on a daily basis - physical, psychological and intellectual.

ANAESTHESIOLOGIST: ARMED FORCES

Anaesthesiologists from armed forces have to play a dual role of professionalism and soldiers officer in the unit. Stressful factors of professionalism are common to the civil medical facilities, however, some specific factors include:

- Fixed forward lethal operation zones.

- Non-standard workplace,

- Difficult situations,

- Innovative equipment.

- Working conditions beyond the control of the individual.

- Phases of production pressure.

- Long working hours without break - Duty medical officer (DMO) – continues to scheduled operation theatre after the night duty in the hospital.

- Army officers duties in the unit.

- Insecurity of leave without relief.

  - member of board proceedings

  - Court of inquiries.

  - Officer's mess responsibilities.

  - Sometimes: officer incharge of medical stores, Quartermaster supply system etc.

  - Sleep deprivation

  - Fatigue - physical and mental.

  - Interpersonal relationship with seniors and juniors.

  - Lack of family accommodation.

  - Fast moving temporary duties.

  - Insecurity of postings and promotions.

  - Lack of opportunities of professional growth and status who's who in the medical society.

BURNOUT SYNDROME:

Burnout syndrome is occupational psychological medical disorder that results from chronic and unmanaged workplace stress. It has three characteristics:

- Energy depletion - exhaustion

- Mental apathy from job or negativism

- Professional inefficiency.

Literally, it means slow smoley fire that turns into ashy hollowness. It can be defined as a sustained uncontrolled stress that leads to the loss of physical and mental energy, emotional and psychological exhaustion and withdrawal.

Physicians develop a sense of guilt of their failure to benefit the humanity. It is disappointment of professional autonomy, doctor-patient relationship, ability to help the patients, and lack of appreciation of their knowledge skills and dedication by other colleagues and society. Some develop workaholic with damage of interpersonal relationship even the closest. Finally their productivity is depressed that further contribute to their development of burnout. It becomes a vicious cycle of sustained constant stress to the level of dissatisfaction, poor performance and premature retirement.

Body protective "General adaptation syndrome", fight or flight" reaction of autonomic nervous system fails to sustained stress. Excessive stress causes adverse effects such as:

Physical illness: Hypertension, coronary artery disease, chronic musculoskeletal pain syndromes, gastritis, spontaneous abortion, depressed immune system.

- Gullette EC, Blumenthal JA, Babyak M, et al Effect of mental stress on myocardial ischemia during daily life JAMA 1997, 277, 152-1526.

- Cohen S, Tyrrell DA, Smith AP, Psychological stress and susceptibility to common cold. N Engl J Med, 1991, 325, 606-612.

- Caippo JT, Berntson GG, Malarkey WB, et al Autonomic neuro-endocrine and immune responses to psychological stress, the reactivity hypothesis. Ann NY Acad Sci, 1998, 840, 664-673.

Emotional deterioration is manifested as

- Anxiety and depression

- Irritability

- Extended fatigue.

- Anger and mood elevation.

- Frustrations.

Behavioral disorders is seen as:

- Inactivity or lack of alert

- Accident proneness

- Impulsive reactions

- Aggressive actions

- Alcoholism

- Substance - chemical abuse.

Intellectual dysfunctions are characterised as:

- lack of concentration

- poor task performance

- forgetfulness

- diminished alertness

◈ Parker JB, The effects of fatigue on physician performance - an underestimated cause of physician impairment - and increased patient risk, can J Anaesth 1907, 34, 489-495.

STRESS IS BENEFICIAL?

Stress is positive to concentrate to focus, achieve optimism, to target the goals, success and efficiency. Stress is necessary to gain in the process of education and training for physicians and even in the medical practice. However, stress represents differently to different people, different situations and at different times. It should never be allowed to the level of exhaustion or detrimental levels. High performance is accompaniment of stress:

- strong commitment and will-power to professionalism.

- positivity and confidence

- Focus with personal sense of achievement.

- Responsibility to self well-being.

- Self-esteem

- access to supportive personal relationship.

- Recognizing and managing stress at an early stage.

ANATOMY OF STRESS:

Stress has three components - the stressor, the psychological filters and the coping responses.

Professional-Environmental and personal stressors

Trigger stressor causes changes of pressure demands and threats to initiate the cycle

Evaluated and processed by psychological filters

(life events, conditioned experiences, belief and expectations, personality, value system - are evaluated)

Stress reactions and coping responses of arousal activating system.

Trigger stressor inadequately processed, and managed, will lead to unresolved stress of end-product to create tension and distress. Any further stress superimposed will compound the effects of distress to cause detrimental health. Stress is always an active process, daily occurrence, daily interactions of the stressors that the individuals come across. It is the dynamic understanding to manage stress and real possibility.

Stressors are always ongoing, a regular part of life. Exceptionally small percentage capture our intention, that is, high intensity and deep personal meaning. Stress process is the change, demand or pressure upon us. We usually find ways to handle these stressors – some beneficial – but ineffective management of low-intensity, daily annoyance and frustrations can be accumulative.

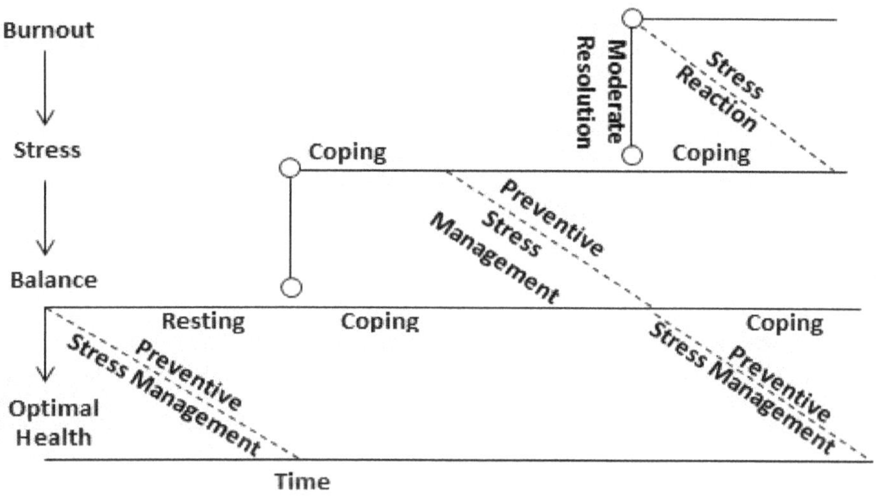

Stages of stress management

Managing routinely, the unavoidable stressors can fortify our determination to fight the superimposed acute high-intensity crisis.

Each one of us lives a state of stable basal level of stress. Each one of us have an absolute threshold level of tolerance of stress beyond which it is burnout and harmful - physical, emotional and psychological. The threshold level is variable for each individual - low, intermediate or high. This level of threshold, the magnitude of difference between the basal and the threshold, determines the margin of safety or the buffer zone. That is called the adaptive reserve against the harmful effects of stress.

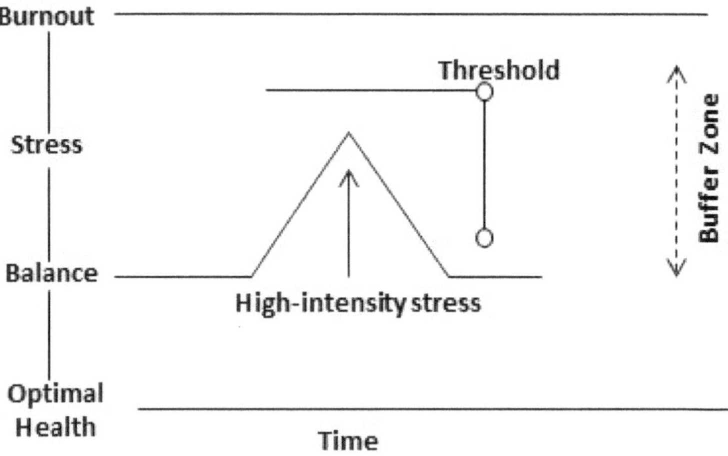

Personality of the individual has been linked to the life-style disorders in medicine. Similarly, those intense behaviour personalities are prone to the stress. These people are framed to hurried time, judgement of others and self-esteem. They fail to achieve self satisfaction, peace of mind and control over their lives. They are always; anxiety, resentment, anger and hostility. They think ahead competitive deadlines next task. They are called "over-achievers" but fail to understand the adverse effects of an uncontrollable stressful lifestyle.

Stress modulation:

Stress is multidimensional of daily walk of life. Stress cycle needs to be culminated with modified stress responses. We can modulate or activate the response with multiple strategies and priorities such as integration of our personal, professional and spiritual domain. We work in the direction of physician culture, particularly, the anaesthesiologists, and the peri-operative medicine.

Firstly, the stress needs to be recognized, measured and evaluated. The most common reasons as precursors to clinical anaesthesia are excessive work hours, sleep deprivation, and fatigue. Loss of sleep causes the disability of mental, psychological and physical burnout syndrome. Sleep biology is multifactorial process associated with physiological and behavioural components. It is biological necessity. Decrement impairs vigilance reaction time, psychomotor coordination, information processing and decision-making. These tasks are paramount to the delivery of clinical anaesthesia in the operating room. Microsleep event is a variant of sleep deprivation disorder, of which, the anaesthetist may be unaware. During this episodic microsleep event, vigilance becomes impossible and impaired performance.

Fatigue causes decreased ability to physical work, cognitive functions, personal motivation, emotional status and psychological well-being. Anaesthesiologists "denigrate and ignore" the adverse effects of sleep deprivation and fatigue. They succumb to the stress of production pressure to work even when knowingly sleep deprived and fatigued. This is the dangerous phenomenon of anaesthesia culture.

Sleep deprived and fatigued anaesthesiologists develop unstable emotional states and start looking for the alternatives to appear fit and healthy. Environmental stimuli, social interaction and drugs caffeine can influence the actual degree of sleepiness or fatigue. They gain access to the chemicals that can influence the level of wakefulness, anxiety and mood, sometimes, self administration of banned drugs becomes the entrance point of chemical dependence. Willful efforts to remain awake and alert when one is sleep deprived and fatigued is highly stressful. Naps even of short duration of 45 mins enhances alertness, judgement, creativity and production.

Status deprivation:

Physicians (Anaesthesiologists) work hard from the days of their educational and training period to achieve status within the medical community and civil society, failure to reach to that level impairs their self-esteem, causes deprivation, victimisation and frustration. It becomes stressful failure of life.

Coping strategies:

Human race has remarkable ability to cope. Life enhancing attitudes and behaviors further facilitate and counterbalance the stresses and strains. It is to experience and strive the target of balance and optimal performance. "Bigger is better" "more is best" syndromes usually lead to burnout and illness, therefore, needs to be rejected. Similarly, "self disregard" is not safe to excellence in achievement, it will cause physical, emotional and intellectual disabilities. Successful stress management may be discussed as:

Self-care

Direct-action

Support relationship

Behavioral situation control

Adaptability-flexibility

Time-pressure management.

Nutrition

Meditation

Positive emotion entertainment.

Self care enhances physical and psychological well-being and endurance. Prevention of illness is invaluable. Self care includes physical exercise, nutrition and hygiene, sleep and rest, distractions and entertainment, family relationship,

Nutrition:

Calorie diet

Nutrition and vitamin supplements

Aspirin low dose 325 mg per day

Personal hygiene.

Immunizations

Avoid pollution

Sleep hygiene-quality

Psychological consequences of stressful anaesthesiologists:

- Anxiety

- Insecurity

- Emotional suppression

- Isolation from peers and family

- relegated to status of lesser worth.

- impaired self esteem.

- feeling of rejection in life

- Depression

HUMANISTIC ANAESTHESIA.

Anaesthesia is the care of the human-life as the knowledge of medicine but more important is emotions, human feelings, spirit and will. It is the individual value and meaning, doctor-patient relationship and support during the critical illness. When anaesthesiologists do not get acknowledgement of their humanistic qualities as physicians, it hurts their consciousness and constitutes a state of personal stress.

Preanesthetic and post anesthetic care are the periods of perioperative interactions that create bonds of patient-doctor relation. It consolidates the perceptions that anaesthetists are caring, skillful, medical professional and trustworthy perioperative physicians. It promotes self-esteem and reputation status.

Meditation is the strategy of self deep relaxation, that promotes rest, release of tension, peace of mind and peace environment.

Relaxation response is related to psychophysiology of stress-free body. Deep breathing, muscle - relaxation and focus attention are the components of relaxation.

Direct action strategy addresses to achieve tasks without confrontation, distraction and straightward responsibility and commitment. Learn to say NO with assertiveness for direct action. Stressful anger and resentment is avoided to build priorities, morale and self-esteem. Support relationship is the most valid strategy to combat stress of professionalism, domestic, social culture and environment. It is to share experiences and belief systems. It needs to create network of relationships as an essential instrument of stress. Professionalism stress can be minimised with good working environment, sharing trust, respect and support of the peers. Success and failure, is part of medicine, sharing of such experiences builds self confidence to reduce stress. Spouse, is the long-term relationship, may be medical or non-medical background, facilitates pleasure and family stress free life. Marriages advance the career achievements of the partners. Conflict marriages are also known but beyond the scope of this write up.

Behavioral situation control strategy is the conflict control avoiding the confusion disagreeable to the parties. One needs to recognize the resolution that benefits to regulate without compromise of expectations and medical care. It help to create stress free situations and peace of mind. It builds confidence and self esteem. Adaptability is the strategy of flexibility in response to the demands of the rigid reactions for managing stressful situations. It needs maturity, patience and wisdom to act.

Time-pressure management is the strategy of priority to the stressors, to be effective efficiently. Anaesthesiologists are the professional experts to workplace time management. They are busy with cognitive minute details in the operating rooms, long hours to work on daily basis, many of them fail to have weekly or monthly vacations at the cost of revenue. Internet technology has overshadowed true leisure - creative or contemplative time to refresh them. Anaesthesiologists need leisure time to rest, relaxation and revitalising activities. Even laughter and humor should never be underestimated as psychological and social fool to combat stress.

Do not suffer from humor impairment - be lighten up, to laugh and playful.

Workplace stress is related to the individual anaesthetists, or combined workforce of anaesthesia, work environment and healthcare organisation "stress-lysis" is the responsibility of all concerned cooperation to mutual benefit, common cause is related to ethics, motivation, safe environment, agreeable situations, fairness to rules, professionalism and economic functions. Present day focus of stress management strategies has shifted from individual work force to environmental or organisations. Individual anaesthetists cannot excel or avoid burnout in a healthcare organisation that creates stress. One needs to watch the delivery of healthcare attitude towards its workers. Self esteem as a requisite of well-being must be acknowledged and respected

- Anaesthesiologists are prone to morbidity and younger mortality (68.98 ± 15.55) years compared to all other physicians (74.41 ± 13.3) years

  - ▲ Jonallian D, Katz MD, Do anaesthesiologists die at a younger age than other physicians? Age adjusted death rates Anaesth:Analg, 2004, 98, 1111-1113.

- High death rate among anaesthesiologists below the age of 45 years as the suicide cause is of concern. Coronary artery disease is the most common cause of death among the anaesthesiologist may be due to the factor professionalism stress. Deaths due to lymphoid and reticuloendothelial system malignancies relate to the toxicity of inhaled anaesthetics or operation theatre environmental pollution.

- ▲ Bruce DT, Eide Ace, Linde WH, et al. Causes of death among anaesthesiologists: A 20 year Survey, Anaesthesiology, 1968, 29, 565-569

- Medical profession no longer commands respect and prestige. Job satisfaction is eroded. Mental and emotional strains are the increasing pressures of lack of time and uncertainty. Anaesthesiologists work with stressful conditions.

  - ▲ Kam PCA, Occupational stress in Anaesthesia. Anaesth. Intens Care, 1997, 25, 686-690.

- Providers are themselves sick - reasons may be productivity pressure, time pressure, expanding medical knowledge, limited opportunities of update medicine, difficulty to balance personal and professional life etc.

  - ▲ Tait Shanafelt, Burnout in anaesthesiology - a call to action. Anaesthesiology, 2011, 114, 1-2.

  - ▲ High incidence of burnout in academic chairs, Anaesthesiology, 2011, 114, 181-193.

  - ▲ Hyman SA, Michaels DR, Berry JM, et al Risk of burnout in perioperative clinicians. A survey study and literature review. Anaesthesiology, 2011, 114, 194-204.

- Acute stress amongst the anaesthesiologists during induction of anaesthesia was revealed with increase in cardiovascular (Heart rate and blood pressure) anxiety state (state trait anxiety inventory - STAI) and salivary cortisol levels. It is the physiological stress during the perioperative period.

  - ▲ Kain NZ, Chan MK, Jonathon D, et al, Anaesthesiologists and Acute peri-operative stress. A cohort study. Anaesth Analg, 2002, 95, 177-183.

  - ▲ Kawasaki K, Sekimoto M, Ishizaki T, work stress and workload of full-time anaesthesiologists in acute care hospitals in Japan. Journal of Anesthesia, 2009, 23, 235-241.

- It has documented that the work stress among anaesthesiologists is related to workload, work environment and no support stress.

- Work and Rest has become an essential pattern of clinical anesthesia. Fatigue induced errors amongst the anaesthesiologists must be prevented for safety to the patients. Fatigue can affect performance, ability to learn and family life.

  ▲ Gravenstein JS; Cooper JB, orkin fk, work and rest cycles in anaesthesia practice. Anaesthesiology 1990, 72, 737-42.

- Anaesthesiologists face stress on being on-call duty is related to ill-health. The symptoms documented were:

Falling asleep during activity

Tearfulness

Feeling guilt

Difficulty verbal speech

Need for alcohol

Arrhythmias

Dyspnea

Nasal congestion

Headache

Memory disturbances

Irritation

Exhaustion.

Stress of on-call workload was positive correlation of exhaustion and burnout. Sick leave and perceived lack of sleep were associated with workload. Magnitude of on-call workload was directly related to mental, behavioral and somatic stress disorder.

▲ Lindfors PM, Nironi KE, Meretoja OA, et al; On call stress among Finnish anaesthesiologists. Anaesthesia 2006, 61, 856-866.

BALANCING CARE: ADDRESSING STRESS AND WELLBEING IN HEALTHCARE PROFESSIONALS

Dr. ICHHA KAUR

SENIOR CONSULTANT

DEPARTMENT OF ANAESTHESIOLOGY, PARAS HOSPITAL GURUGRAM

M.B.B.S: GRANT MEDICAL COLLEGE, J.J. HOSPITAL MUMBAI

M.D. ANAESTHESIOLOGY T.N. MEDICAL COLLEGE AND B.Y.L. NAIR HOSPITAL MUMBAI

HEALTHCARE MANAGEMENT AND PROFESSIONAL ANALYTICS PROGRAMME: IIM KOZHIKODE

Hypocrites oath while foundational in medical ethics primarily focuses on responsibilities of physicians towards their patients. However it lacks provisions to address the challenges that physicians often face. It overlooks the importance of fostering a collaborative environment and camaraderie professionals.

The medical world adopted the declaration of Geneva in 1948 which has been amended several times. The current version of this declaration (2017) recognises the increasing workload, occupational stress and potential adverse effects these have on physicians health and their ability to provide highest standard of care. It also incorporated the idea of reciprocity of respect into the ethical framework of medical profession by adding a statement " I will give to my teachers, colleagues and students the respect and gratitude that is their due. "Close this shift reflects a more holistic approach to medical ethics recognising the human race relational aspect of the profession.

The National Institute For Occupational Safety (NIOSH) describes job stress as the harmful physical and emotional response that occurs when the requirements of the job do not match the capabilities, resources and needs of the workers. Apart from the individual factors the working conditions have direct impact on workforce well-being. This job stress is extremely high in health care professionals due to their demanding and often emotionally charged nature of their work. This is compounded by unrealistic societal expectations of error free and perfect medical outcomes. Some of the common causes of job stress in medical practice are as follows:

TIME PRESSURES

Long working hours with unpredictable schedules. We all are familiar with the scenario when we have had to leave our children's birthday parties or family gatherings to attend to patient emergencies.

LACK OF RESOURCES

Dealing with high patient to staff ratio, untrained staff or lack of equipment to meet the patient's requirement is a daily ordeal. Many times administrative tasks take time away from patient care for example a medical professional may spend hours filling out forms of insurance documentation, discharge summaries while patients wait to be attended.

EMOTIONAL STRAIN

Witnessing suffering in the form of terminal illnesses, trauma, death on a regular basis. There is a constant fear of making medical errors with fatal consequences. Also frequently medical professionals face ethical dilemmas related to end of life care.

INTERPERSONAL CHALLENGES

There is a constant struggle to find work life balance. On the work front medical professionals are constantly dealing with emotionally charged abusive patients and their relatives. Also, this problem is compounded by poor communication between healthcare teams and with administration

SOCIETAL EXPECTATIONS

Society often expects medical professionals to be available around the clock to address everyone's medical concerns. A distant neighbour may feel entitled to interrupt your family time for advice on a trivial matter like a scratch on the hand.

HEALTH RISKS

Constant exposure to illnesses places health care workers at significant physical risk. Constantly navigating hazardous environment containing blood products, radiation and infectious diseases requires relentless vigilance to ensure personal safety. What better example than the Covid pandemic. This often adds to the mental burden leading to burnout and emotional stress.

It is being increasingly acknowledged that the physician needs to care for their own health and well-being to provide optimal health care for others. Some employers believe that they must turn up the pressure on the workers to remain productive and profitable. However, there are many subtle consequences

For employers, it may translate into increased burnout and physical health problems of employees leading to increased absenteeism. They may also face high job dissatisfaction and the attrition rate at these workplaces may eventually be very high. Patients being treated by medical professionals working under such high-pressure conditions may have decreased quality of care due to burnout apathy and judgement errors which may overall lead to poor patient satisfaction.

DOES STRESS HAVE ANY POSITIVE ATTRIBUTES?

Eustress is something that motivates us to enhance a performance, challenges encourage us to step out of her comfort zone leading to personal and professional growth. But such stress should be short lived, typically occurs in manageable amount is not overwhelming our body and mind. Seeing stress as a challenge rather than a threat to be overcome can make it motivational and boost performance like in a sports competition or a difficult surgery.

It indirectly promotes problem-solving and builds creativity and resilience.

HOW TO RECOGNISE STRESS AMONGST PROFESSIONALS?

Frequent complaints of headaches, persistent fatigue, irritability and trouble sleeping or common signs of stress. Individuals may also experience heightened anxiety, feelings of depression and withdrawal from social interactions. In some cases, stress can lead to increased substance abuse with alcohol, stimulants or sedatives as individuals try to cope. Prolonged stress has also been linked to adverse effects on the cardiac health. In the medical field burnout can significantly raise the likelihood of errors, impaired decision-making, reduce empathy and negatively affect the quality of care provided to the patients.

It's important to distinguish stress from exhaustion, as while they are related, they have key differences. Stress is a state of heightened energy where a body is enough fight or flight state whereas in exhaustion we feel drained and lack of energy to engage with our tasks. Exhaustion can stem from many factors other than work like illness, malnutrition or inadequate sleep. In exhaustion, the tasks which were manageable previously seem impossible due to sustained effort or unrelieved stress. Stress can sometimes enhance performance and have positive effects. However, addressing workforce stress proactively can prevent it from escalating to burnout or exhaustion.

Achieving this requires a collaborative effort from both employers and employees to ensure better outcomes for the organisation as a whole.

MANAGING STRESS IN HEALTHCARE

To effectively address workforce stress in a hospital setting a variety of interventions can be implemented at different levels.

Organisationally, improvements in staffing such as hiring adequate nurses or support staff, can help reduce the workload that often lead to burnout. Some days we actually feel that we are mistaken to be super heroes by not only our patience but by our administrators. Some days flexible scheduling, such as offering rotating shifts or the option to work from home when possible can promote better work life balance. Support systems, like employee Assistant programs or peer support groups which provide emotional support should be established. No one understands us better than the person next to us at 3 AM when we are faced with unexpected situations on a 24-hour shift. Keeping calm and carrying on sounds easier than it actually is when a code blue hits during lunch and sometimes you need to share your plight with a colleague who gets it. Professional developmental programmes including training on stress management, mindfulness and resilience can help healthcare workers cope with challenges.

In terms of workplace environment fostering open communication through regular team meetings or feedback sessions allows staff to voice concerns and suggest improvements. Nothing builds camaraderie better than shared frustration. On the other hand, addressing workplace bullying or interpersonal conflicts proactively can help create a more respectful and supportive atmosphere. Ensuring access to necessary resources which may be something like an ergonomic chair that doesn't leave your back feeling like it's been through a marathon helps staff avoid frustration and inefficiencies. Providing up-to-date medical equipment and resources and encourages medical professionals to constantly update their knowledge and skill leading to greater job satisfaction.

On an individual level, encouraging healthcare workers to take regular breaks helps maintain energy levels. Provision for quiet spaces to collect your thoughts and recharge those batteries is vital. Medical professionals must establish clear boundaries around their time to maintain a healthy work life balance. While the nature of health care often demands responsiveness, it is crucial for professionals to recognise that they cannot attend to everyone's needs, especially outside of working hours. Outside of their regular shifts, medical staff should focus solely on emergencies, allowing time for rest and personal recovery. Setting these boundaries is essential not only for personal well-being but also for maintaining long-term effectiveness in providing quality care.

Leadership in the hospital setting plays a pivotal role in stress management. Recognising and validating staff contributions whether through a staff member of the month or a thank you note from the leadership helps in lifting the spirits of the employees. Creating a culture of appreciation and empathy is the key

such as publicly acknowledging the hard work of teens during stressful times like a surge in patient volume or particularly difficult case can boost morale. Encouraging a culture where medical professionals feel safe to acknowledge their mistakes rather than hiding them is essential for fostering a learning environment and improving patient care in medical profession where the pressure to be flawless can be overwhelming but when mistakes are kept hidden it prevents growth and can lead to worse consequences down the line. When there is no blame, anonymous reporting systems Staff feel more comfortable in admitting mistakes. For example, if an anaesthesia technician administers the wrong those of a medication if you feel supported in reporting the mistake immediately the error can be caught and corrective actions can be taken to prevent the harm to the patient. By creating an environment where mistakes are viewed as opportunities for learning hospitals can ensure they are continuously improving patient safety with the focus is on solutions not blame. This approach promotes accountability and strengthens team collaboration leading to better patient care.

We need to address stress at multiple levels-organisational, environmental, individual and at the leadership level to improve not only the well-being of healthcare professionals but also ensuring better outcomes for the organisation as a whole.

WHY ARE OPERATING ROOMS HIGH STRESS ENVIRONMENTS FOR ANAESTHESIOLOGIST?

In many developing countries, the role of the anesthesiologist in ensuring a successful surgical outcome is often underappreciated, both by the general public and within the medical community itself. The surgeon is typically seen as the primary hero in the operating room (OR), while the anesthesiologist is often regarded as a secondary figure, contributing mainly to perioperative care without receiving the recognition they truly deserve. This disparity in perception, coupled with differences in information, values, experience, and priorities between surgeons and anesthesiologists, can lead to conflict in high-pressure environments like the OR. Anaesthesiologist usually have little influence over how surgical procedure is the time than carried out, which is a big factor causing dissatisfaction. Such pressures not only create a negative atmosphere but also contribute to increased stress levels.

A study conducted to evaluate the understanding of paramedical staff about the anesthesiologist's role in patient care revealed concerning results: only 49.20% of the staff recognized that anesthesia is a distinct specialty, and of those, 60% understood that anesthesiologists have a specific role in the OR.

Meanwhile, 35.85% regarded anesthesiologists merely as assistants to the surgeon, and the remaining staff had no clear understanding of what anesthesiologists actually do. This lack of awareness contributes to a diminished sense of self-worth among anesthesiologists, exacerbating the stress they face in the operating room.

Due to a nature of responsibilities there is need for precision and constant vigilance we are responsible for critical decision-making under pressure where misjudgement can lead to life threatening complications. Like many medical professionals, anaesthesiologist may have to work long hours, night shifts or through back to back complicated surgeries. The physical and mental toll of prolonged attention and high-intensity work can increase stress levels contributing to burn out.

Stress in the operating theater is inevitable due to the high-pressure nature of surgical procedures, but it must be managed effectively to ensure the well-being of both medical professionals and patients. The operating theater is a dynamic environment that requires seamless collaboration among multidisciplinary teams, including surgeons, anesthesiologists, anesthesia technicians, scrub staff, blood bank personnel, and ICU teams. Each team member plays a crucial role in ensuring the success of the procedure and patient safety.

To mitigate stress in the operating theater, several strategies can be employed:

1. Pre-operative planning: an anaesthesiologist should perform a detailed preoperative assessment of the patient prior to procedure and have a well-defined plan of Anaesthesia anticipating potential complications. Having this information at hand significantly reduces the stress during procedures

2. Use established safety checklist like WHO surgical safety checklist to ensure that all equipment and instruments are ready and functioning

3. Proper time management and avoiding delays as they can have cascading effects due to rushed procedures decision making adding to the stress. It is Important to brief everyone in the team about the responsibilities so that the surgeries can adhere to the timelines.

4. Long surgeries can lead to mental and physical fatigue so ensuring break for all team members during then the procedures to prevent exhaustion.

5. Seniors in the operating room should maintain a calm and composed demeanour which helps in maintaining a more stress-free and efficient environment reducing the likelihood of mistakes.

6. It is the personal and institutional responsibility that every physician keeps up with latest medical knowledge and procedures in their speciality. This imparts confidence and competence to meet the challenges and provide optimal medical care.

7. Having a encouraging and supportive team can significantly improve performance while reducing stress. A collaborative team ensures mutual respect with the culture of empathy, shared responsibility positive reinforcement and empathy for members. It is a team where everyone is comfortable in sharing their thoughts and ideas openly.

8. Physicians often put their own health on the backburner neglecting self-care. Physical and mental well-being help us better handle the demands of the job. It is important to have adequate rest, proper nutrition, develop hobbies and do regular exercise. It is important to invest time in ourselves and our relationships. Our Health fuels the care we provide and inability to perform our duties well will eventually lead to increased stress.

Let's prioritise our well-being for us, our families and our patients. It has been recognised that health and well-being of the Anaesthesiology workforce is integral to the work we do. In the year 2024-2025 the world Federation of societies of anaesthesiologist (WFSA) has decided to raise awareness about the importance of well-being of the Anaesthesia workforce and the impact it has on the patient care. Like they say in an aeroplane safety briefing it's time to wear our own mask before helping others.

1. Khetarpal R, Chatrath V, Kaur J et al. Occupational stress in anesthesiologists and coping strategies: a review. Int J Sci Stud 2015; 3(6): 188-192.

2. Bhattarai B, Kandel S, Adhikari N. Perception about the role of anesthesia and anesthesiologist among the paramedical staffs: Perspective from a medical college in Nepal. Kathmandu Univ Med J (KUMJ) 2012;10:51-4.

3. Sumitra Ganesh Bakshi, Jigeeshu Vasishtha Divatia, Sadhana Kannan, and Sheila Nainan Myatra, "Work-related stress: A survey of Indian anesthesiologists," Journal of Anaesthesiology Clinical Pharmacology 33, no. 1 (2017): 86-91

4. Maria V. Korehova, Alexander G. Soloviev, Irina A. Novikova, and Mikhail Y. Kirov, "Manifestations of Professional Burnout Syndrome in Anesthesiologists and Resuscitators," Annals of Anesthesia and Pain Medicine 3, no. 1 (2020): 1010,

Brigadier Yudhvir Suri, VSM visit to department of Anesthesiology and critical care, AFMC Pune on 30th August 2024.

Lecture to the faculty and residents:

- We have responsibility to develop the specialty anesthesiology beyond further.

- We are responsible to the younger generation of anesthesiologists.

- We are responsible to the organisation, that is, Armed Forces Medical Services, India.

Younger generation, post-graduates, were advised:

Concept - 1

▲ Speciality before self, (Work place anesthesiology).

Concept - 2

- Utilise the opportunities offered to best of your career.

Concept - 3

- Allow the administration cell to decide your future.

Concept - 4

▲ Deliver to the soldier.

During the interaction with the residents with informal tea, it was stressed that we need to deliver to the soldier, as the fundamental principle of medical delivery system in the Armed forces India and further, it was deliberated, do not ask administration "pump-postings" (postings to the commands or super speciality centers) but **render your services best to the patient, may be the remote field, best to your careers. Your remote field service becomes the History in Indian Military Medicine.**

Brigadier Yudhvir Suri, VSM with faculty and residents, (seen Professor HOD Air Comdr. Aditya Sapra, Colonel Bhardwaj, Major Jaimni Joy and residents) on 30th August 2024, at AFMC Pune.

Brigadier Yudhvir Suri, VSM was presented a momento by Air Comdr. Aditya Sapra, HOD and Colonel Bhardwaj Associate Professor, department of Anesthesiology, Armed Forces Medical College, Pune on 30th August 2024

Honour of Excellence, teacher's trophy: Anesthesiologists, BJMC Pune:

Brigadier Yudhvir Suri, VSM was invited to commemorate professor (Dr.) AM Deshpande. oration delivered by Professor (Dr.) Ramesh, an eminent pediatric anesthesiologist from Chennai (Tamil Nadu)

India on 31st August 2024 during Society of anesthesiologists Pune Conference held at Yashada auditorium Rajbhavan Complex airport road Pune. It was an honour, probably, first time in the history of medicine that a student (Brigadier Yudhvir Suri) speaks to honour his teacher (Professor AM Deshpande). It was an opportunity to present Honour of Excellence teacher's trophy to the faculty residents and all those from BJ medical college, Pune and veterans of that institute at Pune. Our visit to Pune was the reminder of the past at the military complex AFMC Pune (1972 – 1974), MH (CTC) (1986 – 1990) and MH Khadke (1974 – 1977) and now after 35 years. It revived the military culture with our stay at officer's mess MH (CTC) with excellent hospitality from 29 August to 01 September 2024. Meeting friends with whom shared the time of pleasure and crisis at workplace and social environment has been an honour.

Honour of Excellence Professor (Late) A M Deshpande MBBS, DA, MD Teacher's Trophy B J Medical College, Pune Department of Anesthesiology	From: Brigadier Yudhvir Suri, VSM Indian Military Medicine 31st August 2024

Brigadier Rajan RS an eminent Cardiothoracic surgeon, Mrs. Rajan are seen with Mrs. Indu Suri and Brigadier Yudhvir Suri, VSM

Quiz World Anesthesia Day 2024

L → R: Brigadier Yudhvir Suri, Dr. VK Kapoor, Dr. HH Dash, Dr. Prem Nath Kakar, Dr. Baljit Singh and back – ground delegates.

Brigadier Yudhvir Suri, (along with Dr. Apra Rai and Shruti Gupta addressing the delegates of the conference, World Anesthesia Day 2024

Brigadier Yudhvir Suri Champion Trophy Post-graduates Anesthesia Quiz, **World Anesthesia Day, 16 November, 2024**

Seen in the photograph Colonel (Dr.) DK Sharma, HOD anesthesia presenting the trophy, Dr. Arneja Ruchi secretary ISA Gurugram, Dr. Apra Rai and Dr. Shruti Gupta coordinator Quiz

PARAS HOSPITAL	**Dr. Hariltha**	
Sector 54, Suncity	**Dr. Shyma**	**WINNERS**
Gurugram		

Quiz Participants 2024: Residents:

Paras Hospital:

    Dr. Hariltha

    Dr. Shyma

Artimis Hospital:

    Dr. Anjana

Dr. Nandani

SGT Medical College & Hospital:

Dr. Parth

Dr. Divya

Medanta Hospital:

Dr. Sai Deepika

Dr. Saneha

Quiz World Anesthesia Day 2024

Dr. Apra Rai, Senior Consultant anesthesiology, Dr. Shruti Gupta and Dr. Ruchi Sardana, coordinators of the post-graduate Anesthesia

TEAM PARAS TEAM MEDANTA

TEAM ARTEMIS TEAM SGT

Dr. Haritha, Dr. Sai Deepika, Dr. Anjana, Dr. Parth, Dr. Shyama, Dr. Sneha, Dr. Nandani, Dr. Divya

Dr. KL Garg

Consultant anesthesiologist presented lifetime achievement award, World Anesthesia Day, 2024 by Professor Dr. Baljit Singh

Dr. Prem Nath Kakar

Lifetime achievement award by society of Anesthesiologists Gurugram by Professor Dr. HH Dash on World Anesthesia Day 2024.

L to R: Dr. Priyanka, Dr. DK Sharma, Dr. Vijay Vohra, Dr. Ruchi

Life time achievement award to Dr. Vijay Vohra – 2024 Medanta Hospital

5

SOLDIER RELIGION AND SPIRITUALISM

WHAT ELDERS SAID...

◈ **1503 -1566**

◈ **Michael Nostradamus**

Hinduism will become the ruling religion of Europe. The famous metropolis of Europe is the Hindu Capital.

- 1749-1832.

- Bohan Keith

If not today, one day we will have to accept Hinduism because that is the true

Religion.

- **1828 - 1910**

- **Leo Tolstoy**

Hinduism and Hindu will one day rule this world because it is a mixture of knowledge and wisdom.

- **1919**

- **Houston Smith**

Hindutva is not more trusting than we have in ourselves. If we can turn our thoughts and hearts towards Hindutva, it will benefit us.

- **1841-1931**
- **Costa Loban**

Hindus only talk about peace and reconciliation. I invite Christians to praise, change and believe it.

- **1846-1946**
- **Herbert Wells**

How many generations are going to face the atrocities and murders until Hinduism is well understood.

Only that day, the world will become a place for humans to settle and live.

- **1856-1950**
- **Bernard Shaw**

One day this world will accept Hinduism. Refusing to accept the true name of Hinduism will only make one accept its principles. Western nations will surely one day convert to Hinduism. The religion of the learned is equal to that of Hinduism.

- **1879 - 1955**
- **Albert Einstein.**

He (?) does what the Jews cannot do. He (?) did it with knowledge and energy. But only Hinduism has the power to lead to peace.

- **1872-1970**
- **Bernard Russel**

I read about Hinduism I feel that this is the religion of mankind all over the world.

Hinduism spread throughout Europe, many scholars studying Hinduism will appear in Europe.

One day the situation will develop where only Hindus will lead the world.

Soldiers can belong to any religion they want as long as, it is not illegal under civil law and is compatible with values and standards of the Army. Chaplain were traditionally Christian force to minister the religious – related services to the military. They were specific religion or faith group but worked with military soldiers of all faiths. In 1796, the parliament of Great Britain passed the Royal warrant that established the military chaplains ministry in the British Army. USA military chaplains served as officers in the US Armed Forces uniform with promotion and rank structure. They wore cleric attire only on duty of religious service. Similarly, all militaries, the world – over had the services of chaplains to serve the soldiers and their families.

Indian Army is a secular organization, officers and all other ranks serve the nation with pride irrespective of their religion, caste, creed or gender.

- *(PIT: Govt. of India, MOD, Indian Army proud of secular credentials).*

Indian Army values loyalty, duty, respect, selfless service, integrity, nation before self. 80 to 85% are Hindus, 15 to 19.5 Sikhs and the rest are the minorities such as Muslims and Christians. Sikhs predominantly are in Sikh regiments, Sikh light infantry, Jammu – Kashmir light infantry, Punjab regiments, Para – units and other battalions that have mixed soldiers Hindus, Sikhs, Jats, Muslims and other minorities.

The military is an arm of the government, may not endorse the form of religion. Enforcement of the constitutional principles must come from the higher authorities and filter down the chain of command. Constitution of India, guarantees the religious freedom to its citizens similar to Americans religious rights of freedom.

A soldier is a person who is a member of an army. A soldier can be a conscripted or volunteer enlisted person, a non – commissioned, warrant officer or an officer.

Sometimes, individuals are compelled by force or law in times of war that is called conscription or a draft. Many countries in the world have enforced registration or law that applies to young males extendable to females or the non – citizens as well. It is need based of the country defence forces. Enlistment of the soldiers is volunteer based on motivation, remuneration and normative incentives.

PHYSICIAN TO ARMY BY FAITH

Soldiers, more so, the physicians – to the medical care, used to join the fighting force by loyalty to the family, friendship, and faith. (Mid, 18th century Jacobite Vs British Army). British army service in mid, 18th century was not an attractive career option for qualified doctors or surgeons. Regimental surgeon were poorly paid and unlike combatant officer colleagues did not have other private means. Some physicians even took the combatant commission to boost their income. The practice of combatant commission to physicians was stopped in 1780.

The title of "Exempt from bearing Arms in Battle is taken from the 1567 letter of exemption given to Edinburgh surgeons by Mary Queen of Scots which excused the physicians from carrying arms; Royal college of surgeons of Edinburgh of special collections, letter of exemption, accessed 2021.

- *Barnsley, RE; The life of an 18th century army surgeon. Journal of the society for Army Historical Research Vol. 44 No. 179, 1966 P 131 – 134.*

The status of commissioned surgeon of the army ranked below the youngest ensign, many regimental medical officers entered the service before they were properly initiated in the principles of their profession, that is, internship. It was not uncommon to list as a surgeon's associate and progress to regimental surgeon based on experience alone with no further formal training. It was the basic qualification in medicine recruitment without formal training as associate or assistant to the regimental surgeon.

DIVERSITY

India is known of diversity, culture, linguistic, religion, demographic. The brilliant philosopher Sarvepalli Radhakrishnan, 2nd President of independent India agreed unity in diversity, the phrase often used in modern India. Heterogenous structure of India contains more than one fifth of world's population (1.40 billion, 20%) that is extraordinarily diverse both religiously and linguistically. India has approximately 800 million Hindus, 200 million Muslims (third largest Muslim population in the world) 24 million Christian, 20 million Sikhs, 10 million Buddhists, 4 million Jains, 6 million others Zoroastrians, Jews and Bahai. 700, 000 others do not mention of their religion.

This is not to mention linguistic diversity which includes Hindi, Bengali, Telugu, Marathi, Tamil, Urdu, Gujrati, Kanada, Sanskriti and more than 558 dialects. Indian civilization has faced disastrous conflict of social. economic and legal inequality long before the wars within the Christianity in Europe and consequent development of secularism as a political solution. In such diverse environment, people need to find solutions for living together that is based on distribution of power, a modus vivendi. The challenge still remains in the environment where religion seems so pervasive.

The religious doctrines, rituals and practices are exclusive. Similarly, political and scientific comprehensive doctrines are exclusivist. However, the adherent ethics of good life flows from such road of truth, means to achieve enlightenment, salvation. There are multiple doctrines which are incomplete in diverse society that is the cause of potential disastrous conflict. Human mind is not immune to such influences of the society, more so, during the young age. The resource of soldiers of Armed forces India is civil society.

Hinduism, Buddhism, Islam and Sikhism are main exclusivist religious traditions in South Asia. They cover every aspect of follower's life Christianity in Europe is conceptual in character, that separates God from individualism. Traditional Indian citizens, or ordinary villagers in India are grounded in comprehensive religious doctrines. However, tolerance, respect and peaceful cohabitation is the order of the day. Indian History describes the periods of Ashoka, Akbar, Kabir and Gandhi as the examples of toleration and respect to the religion.

Religious extremism and violence is increased during post – independent India. Is it an indicator of modernity or liberalization. Is it the political power supporting the Hindu Nationalist movements? Is the old Hindu nationalist movement such as Hindu Mahasabha activated to new political conception of Hindutv? Rashtriya Swayam Sevak Sangh (RSS) has supported the non – congress political government platform to integrate the religious rituals and traditions at various institutions including the Armed Forces India.

Hindutva is no match to Vedic texts nor a place for religious institutions in judiciary or compulsory, religious education or censorship of science in the name of religion. Actually, the Hindutva movement has become the "Religious" voice in the society to subdue the secular credentials of the Constitution of India. It appears that Hindutva is the instrumentation of religion for the use of political power. Some people have given the name to this new trend of communalism by modernity secularization and private religious realm. One needs to understand the distinction of religion, faith, way of life and ideology.

India's religious diversity and domestic politics had complexities to impact the Indian Armed Forces. The constitution of India paved the rigorous path ahead. The foundation of secular outlook was rooted in the embracement of encultured notion that the military institution had no religion and the equivalent of holy book was the constitution.

Loyalty to constitution and fighting spirit of soldier are pillars to the Armed forces. Institutional loyalty to constitution is the paramount of military leadership while the religious identity to deliver the fighting spirit is expected to transcend through faith in God.

Soldier faith is the courage and strength to face the difficult situation and condition of the battlefield that threatens to their physical survival and mental stability. It is blind faith in personnel God of the individual that pushes their fighting capabilities in war. This is a cultural proclivity that has evolved through the military heritage over years in the past.

Cultural proclivity of the Armed forces India has been shaped by colonial heritage. The organization structure was based on religion, caste, region and ethnicity. It supported the British rule policy of "Divide and rule". After independence of more than seven decades, the Indian Army still retains the structure organization and composition of its combat such as infantry, Armored Corps, Mechanized Infantry, Artillery and Engineers. (Author Brig. Dr. Yudhvir Suri VSM had the honour to serve Armored and Engineers as regimental medical officer)

Restructure of army organization to an all India class, composition has failed in the name of Tradition. Sikh Units mutinied during the "Blue star operations" to clear the Golden Temple of terrorists in 1984. There is questionable notion that fighting spirit is better realized when unit and regimental cohesion is built on commonalities such as religion, caste, region, and ethnicity. Religious polarization and its, implication have been sweeping the Indian political landscape since Babri demolition in 1992. It has further deteriorated and deepened across the length and breadth of Indian Society. It is understandable that the human mind of the Armed Forces could also be infected by the polarizing forces that pose a threat to their secular and a - political character.

Lieutenant General MK Katiyar GOC – in – C Western Command said on 13 January 2021 "what makes the Indian Army stand out is that we strictly adhere to the important principles, the first one being our secular approach and the second our a - political character. It means we respect all religions and stay clear of politics. It was well understood in the social media that compromise on these principles will hurt the Army," (Western Command website Army). However, such voices were not tolerated to the ruling dispensation.

Manifestations of cultural stuffs in the institutional character of the military are best identified by the military leadership. These manifestations are reflected in the values, rituals, heroes, and symbols that are embraced. Armed Forces prohibit religious articles and marks for personnel in uniform. These include:

- Tilak (forehead mark)

- Vibhuti (sacred ash)

- Sacred threads and chains around the neck

- Thread worn on the waist

- Tattoos marks

- Specific regard to woman jewellery such as mangal sutra, nose pins and ear rings.

Specific watch is needed to implement these instructions strictly. These signs could reflect the deeper trends impacting the cultural values within the Armed Forces.

Violations of symbolic restrictions are easily curbed through personal examples and strict imposition of orders upholding the Army secular and a - political character is the responsibility of the military top leadership. Military leaders should be willing to sacrifice their careers to protect core institutional values, the struggle to with - stand the internal political onslaught of religious polarization.

Religion:

Religion is the belief in God and the activities connected with this. It may be socio-cultural system, designated behaviours, ritual practices, morals, belief, ethics or organizations. It may relate to humanity, super natural transcendental and spiritual elements. It has sacred history, narrative or mythology that might be, preserved in oral traditions, sacred texts, symbols, holy places to expalain the origin of life, universe or nature. There are an estimated 10,000 organized religions including atheists and agnostics, however, Christianity, Islam, Hinduism including Sikhs, Jains and Buddhists account 77 percent of the world population. The remaining are the regional religious identities.

Religion is human beings relation to that which they regard as holy, sacred, absolute, spiritual, divine or worthy of reverence. It consists of way of life, its concerns and fate after death. Scholars have failed to arrive at the suitable sustainable, systematic, comprehensive definition of the religion acceptable to all worldwide.

Spiritualism:

Spiritual means, "thoughts or belief," rather than bodies or physical experience. In other words, spiritual values the imagination, non-material or metaphysical. Spirituality is derived from Latin word spirit, that means the thing that animates life – anything beyond physical existence, from ghost spirits to religious feeling. Spirituality involves the recognition of a feeling or sense or belief that there is something greater than myself something, more "to being human" than sensory experience that the greater – whole of which we are part is cosmic or divine in nature. Spirituality explores the universal themes such as love, compassion, altruism, life after death, wisdom and truth, knowledge of saints, enlightened individuals manifested supernatural men or aspiring to manifest as part of life. It is the discipline to make progress through prayer, ritual and meditation – usually a teacher or mentor is recommended to achieve the end – results.

Spiritualism is the belief that spirits of the dead can communicate with the living, being. It is postulated that the spirits of the dead residing in the "spirit world" of the dead have the ability or inclination to communicate with the living being. The philosophy explains that there exists an immaterial reality that is beyond the reach of the sensory organs. Traditionally, a religious process, to discover the original shape of man, that is, oriented at the "image of God." However, in modern world, spirituality denotes the mental aspect of life as opposed to the material and sensual aspect of life. It is described as the social religion, so called, against the possession of material world, purity of motives, affection, intensions, inner dispositions, way of simple life, devoted to the higher and lower forms of humanity. Higher forms of humanity is explained the invisible (spirit). Some scholars describe spiritualism as the religion of the masses in a limited manner.

6

SOLDIER RELIGION

Do we need a religion in Armed Forces, if yes, then what kind of religion, saffron or non – saffron? S Radhakrishnan, revered President of India, said, "religion is a thought concept to the system," if that fails, the system declines. Thought concept relevant to the Armed Forces is fighting spirit, if that fails, the cause of devotion fails. When religious system is capable of responding to the new challenges, may be from within or from outside, it is healthy and progressive. The need of a religion is devotion to a cause and that cause is existence for the Armed Forces. Religion is neither powerful nor hate. It is based on the principles of secular ideologies, love and brotherhood. Religion supports the simplicity of spiritual life they may decline if it fails. Therefor, religion is needed to value the system.

In crisis moments of life, poor – orphaned situations, God makes us realise that the period of distress and sorrow in the world are temporary, the incidents are a greater part o drama which will end in power, glory and love. The Upanishads declare "if there were no spirit of joy in the Universe who could live and breathe in this world of life." Soldiers firmly believe the writings of these scriptures because they face the dangerous situations more frequently than their civilian counterparts.

- S Radhakrishnan Indian Religions. UBN 079025 Vision Book Pvt. Ltd. 1979 Page 5 – 47: Indian religious thought.

Religion is not superstitions, black – magic or witchcraft and quackery. Neither it is the rituals of bead necklaces, rosaries, triple paint on forehead, ash on body, pilgrimages, holy river baths, meditation, image worship that does not purify a man as service of fellow – creatures does or comrades do in the field. Saffron change does not help the system. Regimentation and traditions are the values o the system relevant to the Armed Forces. No saffron change is accepted to dilute the cause of devotion, the fighting spirit of the soldier.

Hinduism insists "Ahinsa" as in other Indian origin religions, Buddhism and Jainism. This concept prevents the soldier to be effective in the battlefield. We have no Krishna Avatar to bring him out from this dilemma. Non – violence does not appeal to the soldier – religion when the soldier faces the enemy – kill or be killed.

Each religion is a doctrine, worship, uniqueness and individuality of its own. It changes in response to the needs of the age or time. Then why not to have the doctrine of soldier – religion. It is the fellowship of the soldier's spirit, experience, humanity and humanitarian common essences of mankind.

It is an age of humanism. Religion which is insensitive to social corruption or ills, hatred, discard, disintegration, unity coherence understanding is against the welfare of the society. Soldier is community that needs to be protected with the new concept of soldier religion.

Man's evolution is bound with his conscious deeds. Man is an unfinished product, he grows to regenerate, growth permits the life to flow in him. Those who have evolved, excel in their talent, skills and deeds, become exemplary to others, sometimes, penetrate to become history. That is what happens to the soldier, a patriot from citizen.

Man, always stands between the visible and invisible worlds. Religion may teach us the level of consciousness to attain the highest mode of experience, the enlightenment. What soldier desires the ultimate experience of soldiering – to win the war or defeat the enemy.

Religion teaches us, fulfillment of man's life, raised to its highest extent, every aspect of his being. What is needed is re – bornness, an inner evolution, a change in understanding, that is soldiering.

Soldier is a new religion. It is the social integrity that develops in the barracks and training ground of those who have variable background of caste, creed, belief, traditions, culture, language, rituals, personal God and way of life. It the way of life, care and concern, single thought, Nation first and Nationalism.

There were hundred version of each soldier that becomes one version of hundred as the soldier religion. It evolves life long personal religion, everywhere looking for self, creating their path and distinction of future. Prayers, rituals, scripture recitation, kirtan sabhas, of the society were put to rest in cupboard with new enthusiasm of service to the motherland. Religion did not mean, "accidental birth", Hindu, Muslim, Sikh, Parasi, Saini, Buddhist or agnostic. It transformed the kind of faith to live, emotional faith one is born with rituals of upbringing, army did not interfere in the emotional religious upbringing but never promoted the five pillars of all religion:

1.   Belief in God that hurt the humanity.

2.   Reverence of founders of religion that produce hatred.

3.   Scriptures that cause harmony disturbances.

4.   Worship places to discourage fundamentalism.

5.   Rituals to prevent exploitation of ignorance (Brahminism)

The code of conduct is never discuss religion, the topics that appear critical and negative. One God, the creator, preserver and destroyer, omniscient, omnipotent and omnipresent, benign and merciful to the faithful is admitted as the soldier's religion. All religions document that God created the world and there will be an end to all life. Good or bad deeds will result the cycle of rebirth or salvation (Moksha) whereas Muslims (Judeo – Christian – Muslims) will rise from the graves be judged for good or evil in life and accordingly be sent to heaven or hell. However, these are presumtions probably, to reform the society. Religious teachers, scholar, social scientists' avatar have failed to answer life after death concept. There is no debate on the concept of God, good or evil deeds, and the life after death in the soldier religion. Nor the founders of the religion are discussed except that those who formulated the doctorines did good to the humanity nothing more than that. Guru Nanak and many religious reformers of Arya Samaj proclaimed God to be "Nirakar" (formless) and forbade the worship of idols later the similar groups adopted the rituals contrary to the preachings of the enlightened personages. Places of worship may be the emotional medicine to the communities but corrupt Brahminism exploited the poor masses. Bullah Shah, a religious Sufi poet said:

Masjid ddhaa dey, Mandar ddhaa dey

Ddhaa dey jo kucnh ddhenda.

Ik kisey da dil na ddhavein

Rabb dilaan vicch rehndaa

(Break down the mosque, break down, the temple Break down whatever there is besides; But never break a human heart, that is where God Himself resides

Prayers and meditation are not the alternative to the hard work as said by Swami Vivekananda. Empty stomach can not get peace of mind through prayers or rituals nor any one have right to impose religiosity on others. Prayers and meditation is not the curriculum of soldier religion. Kushwant Singh, writer, scholar has written in his book,

"Religion"; coined a motto for modern India. "Work is worship, but worship is not work". He further said, do not waste time, time is God. The concept of "Sanyas," retirement and vanaprastha (renouncement) should be totally rejected. It is suggested to continue to work till one can physically able to do so. Guru Nanak emphasized the work culture in three commandments

Kirt Karo

Naam Japo

Vand Chako

(Work, worship and give in charity)

Khat ghaal

Kiech hatthon dey

Nanak raah pacchaney sey

(He who earns, and gives some of it away, O! Nanak, he has found the right way.)

Soldier religion, similarly, favour good way of life and contribution materially to the society. Soldiers are always at the forefront to serve the mankind – humanity at disaster situations in India. Soldier religion have a vision of the future, serve the motherland, serve the humanity, by planning and implementing, the policies integral to the society welfare. Preserve the environment for the safety of future generation.

Jammu is a city of faith – Hindu, Muslims, Jainism, Sikhism. We have celebrated Id, festivals, Jain Sabas and Guru Langar's. People have blind religious faith in vaarts to support the welfare of family, children and husband. Every mohalla has a Hindu temple and many areas in the city has the professional horoscope spiritual expert. These experts used to treat the medical problems with their black magic. Traditional religious melas, kirtan satsangs, Gita congregations, Ram Lela's, Dushera and Diwali, used to be enjoyed by majoriteans. All those who joined the military service had the back ground influence of religion.

Jaummuiates and devotees from all parts of India have been visiting the Maa Vaishnodevi shrine, myself started to pilgrimage at the age of 12 years, there-after, yearly visits and even early period of my joining the army. Last we had the privilege to visit on last day of my retirement, that is 20 May 2002. Military has provided one section of mule regiment at the base camp Katara – Udhampur district of Jammu to facilitate the army personnels for visiting the 16 kms uphill track of Vaishnodevi. Similarly, army has provided the logistic facilities at Amarnath (Kashmir), Buda Amarnath Poonch (Jammu region), Badrinath, Hemkund Sahib and many other places worshiped by Hindu population.

Soldier religion is adopted by all soldiers, officers and other ranks, but army cares the sentiments of emotional faith of the troops, therefore, the logistics are provided at the religious places to facilitate their visit. Except logistics, it neither support nor interfere in the concept of personal God, personal religion, rituals, prayers and meditation.

Background faiths

Those who visit Amarnath – recite Baba Amarnath Ki Jai or Om Namah Shivaya – it is one of the very powerful mantras. It builds energy in the human system and clears the environment. These words are important Na – Ma – Shiva – Ya as these five words indicate the five elements. Earth, water, fire, air and Ether.

Om is the sound of the universe. Om means peace and love, when there is peace love and harmony in the five elements, there is bliss and joy, chanting the mantra, Om Namah Shivaya can change the effects of planets of the horoscope.

Nandisvara (Nandi) is the symbol vahana and dharma, that simply means righteousness or truthfulness. It connects the infinite consciousness with the innocent consciousness of the mankind.

Nandisvara – Balswroop – sometimes, shown as, milking the mother represents the concept of creation and generation, vitality, virility. Nandi and Linga are integrated worshipping the lord Shiva – vitality fertility, creation, regeneration, cattle and women. Nandisvra, the buffalo vehana concept of lord Shiva has been the spiritual scene of the past civilization.

Concept Balswroop Nandisvara: creation and generation, vitality and virility

Trishul is the spiritual symbol of lord Shiva, that, represents the deity as the healer. Shul means problems or suffering, tri means three, the types of pain that arise in life: physical, spiritual and ethereal. What relieve the suffering is Trishul and it is the hand of Lord Shiva that holds Trishul.

Trishul signifies the nature as Rudra is conceived to three seasons, summer – rain – winter; Lord of universe, above the three conscious states – walking, dreaming, sleep yet upholds these three states, represents Agni, Sun and Air, master of Heaven, Space and Earth; represents three Gunas – Satva, Rajas, Tamas – the divinity is beyond the three Gunas that it holds these together.

Trishul (Trident) signifies the three aspect of God, as Lord Shiva; the creator, the destroyer, the regenerator.

Trishul is the brand symbol of Sangamas – the sect of Shiviates.

Trishul is conceived to Rudra, violent hostile deity yet the supreme healer, complete recovery to the sick, execution of old – age and pains.

Trishul is conceived on the fact that three mothers – Ambika, Durga and Kali – are worshiped as the mother Goddess – the concept of father God and mother Goddess denoting Shiva – Shakti. Shivaism is centered around the power of Shakti that promotes their expansion. Devotees worship linga - yoni as the principle of generative fertility deities combined together.

Trishul represents the God destruction – generating power worshiped. It also symbolized the God of protection. It symbolized both the **God of death – Mahakal – playing the dance of destruction and simultaneously, known to vanquish death as Mrityunjay.** Yama – the lord of death – is documented in Rigveda with absolute powers of destruction. **Shiva – Panchanan is the most eminent of physicians.** The Jalasa, is the remedy of medicinal value called "Gaomaeza" a ritual to be cow's urine. Soma the elixir of immortality that cured and even raised the dead. Soma Rudra, the plant in Munjavat mountains, drives away many incurable diseases.

Shiva rescued Chandra the curse of Daksha – the king of devas of that time. Chandra had to be placed on the head of Shiva to allay the burning heat of poison which he had drunk during the churning of the ocean.

Shiva adopted the celestial river Ganga in his matted hair to check the impact of her fall, allowed her to flow to the sea and purify the ashes of the mortal remains on the earth. It was the spiritual relief to the ancestors and mortal relief to the bereaved ones.

Many people asked me the significance of symbol – Damaru and Behbuti – of the Shaiviates.

Damaru, depicted with lord Shiva, the rhythmic beats of Damaru represents the primal sound of creation, symbolizing the continuous cosmic vibrations that give rise to the Universe.

Bahbuti, smear of ash on the body signifies the transient nature of life and inevitability of death. It reminds the impermance of material pursuits and the ultimate reality that lies beyond the physical realm.

Soldiers have their individual background of religion, personal God, rituals and traditions of worship. Religion and worship remains the personal affair of each soldier. However, Armed Forces provides emotional support of religion to each soldier. It provides infrastructure and facilitates their visit to the selective religious places. Majority of the soldiers undertake religious tourism without understanding the complexities of the religion. It is the emotional adventure of life. Soldier's religion evolves in each soldier as he matures in soldiering and way of life.

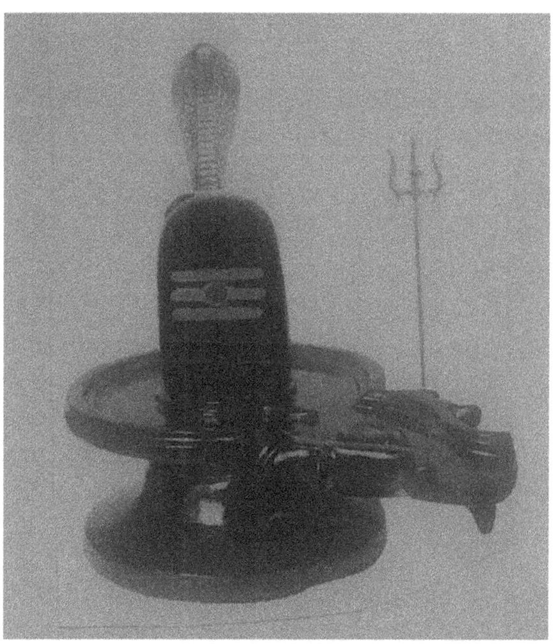

Concept Linga, Trishul, snake represents

lord Shiva as deity healer of mankind.

Vaishno Devi (Trikuta Hills)

The three icons – Maha Kali, Maha Laxmi and Maha Saraswati – all images of Vaishno Devi are worshipped at the temple. The feet of Pindi images are washed by the water brought from the perennial flowing river "Banganga"

Vaishno Devi, combined "tridevi" Shakti, Durga, has the power of entire creation, also called Mahadevi. North – Indians name the shrine "Sheranwali", the loin rider, as the exclusive deity to worship.

The temple, at a height of 1585 metres (5200 ft. ASL) is 16 km. from Katra on the Trikuta hill. It is 65 Km. from Jammu city. The holy cave appears to be nearly one million years old.

Trikuta hill in Rigveda, is the place where temple is located. The Mahabharata, narrate the Kurukshetra war, mention the worship of Goddess Vaishno Devi by Arjuna by the advice of Lord Krishna for blessings. Pleased by devotion and prayers of Arjuna, Maa Vaishno Devi appeared, Stotra, praised by Arjuna - Shloka goes by saying "Jambooka tak chityishu Nityam Sannihitlaye" which means "you who always dwell in the temple on the slopes of the mountains in the Jambhu (present day Jammu). Maa Vaishno Devi Shrine is ancient antiquity as old as pre – Mahabharat. Arjuna worships Vaishno Devi and says, her, the "highest yogi who is free from de restitude and decay, mother of the Vedas, science of dedanta, benefactor of victory, and personification of victory itself." Pandavas were the first to build temples at Kol Kandoli and Bhawan in reverence and gratitude for the mother Goddess. On the mountain, adjacent to the Trikuta hill, over – looking the Holy cave, are the five stone structures which are believed to be the rock symbols of the five Pandavas.

History document that Vaishno Devi temple was in existence by 1846 when Maharaja Gulab Singh established the Dharmarth Trust to manage several temples in his territory. The trust remained in the hands of the Gulab Singh descendants after Independence of India. Dr. Karan Singh was responsible to administer the temple as the hereditary trustee until 1986 when Jagmohan then Governor of Jammu & Kashmir passed legislation transferring control of the Vaishno Devi temple from Dharmarth Trust. Hereditary priests lose the control over the donotions and were brought under the Shrine Board regulations.

Vaishno Devi worship dates back to the time of Indus Valley civilization around 3000 BC. Legend story says that Pandit Shridhar discovered the holy shrine cave around 1000 years ago. Maa Vaishno Devi came to Shridhar in his dream, directed him the reality, direction and location of her cave. Shridhar was an enthusiastic follower of Goddess, started search and eventually traced to the cave.

Originally, there was one natural tunnel for entering and exit of the cave. It was an experience to squeeze through the mountain heads, foot on the flowing Banganga travel zig - zag pathway, to reach for "darshan – Pindi" smooth stone, svarupa, manifestation of Goddess Tridevi – Mahalaxmi, Mahakali and Maha Saraswati. All throughout, there used to be emotional chant of "Jai Mata Di", never any kind of fear inside the cave, time spent inside the holy shrine, was never felt but enlightened the devotees.

It is the "struggle of joy" to reach the sacred shrine. Children, young and old, overcome all odds to receive the blessings of the Goddess. Earlier days, it was 16 km. rough foot tract or one could venture the steep climb of the hills trek. Pony ride or manual baggy were used by the frail, infirm and elderly. There used to be rest - area at dedicated places such as Banganga, Charan Paduka, Adhkwari, Sanjhi – Chhat before reaching the holy cave.

It is interesting that Adhkwaari and Sanjhichhat have the hill hike – up stations. The devotees squeeze through the cave with triple image of the Goddess seen at the end. This ritual of crawl symbolizes "Gestation and Birth", although to Goddess is known to be virgin. Climbing the trek and rituals enroute is the part of the challenge of the sacredness of the pilgrimage.

1977, another tunnel was created to facilitate the smooth entry and exit from the cave without squeeze through the mountain heads and zig – zag pathway. This cave is 100 feet long at 5200 ft. ASL.

1998, third cave was created to facilitate "Entry and Exit separate," to the devotees. However, God and Goddesses, fill the cave to greet the pilgrams, emotional chants of :Jai Mata Di", dedication and wading through a pool flowing water, takes the devotees to the climax, manifested Pindis, for darshan and out of the cave.

It is interesting to recollect that trekking of 16 Km. was the end to refresh under the snow – cold water of the bathing ghat before joining the queue for darshan of the Holy deity pindis. After the darshan "Dhaba lungar" was body freshening for down – trek to Katra.

Soldiering as well as life are the rare opportunities to self – attainment. It is the "call of reality" to wrest the immortal from mortal. It is the "call of awakening" for the soldier in the battlefield. It is selfless cause to the society and the nation. Religion is the binding force of solidarity to the soldier which will deepen the cause to the human society. It is called the soldier religion.

Soldier learns to "stop the wheel of imagination" and "act to the situation." Soldiering is an intelligence of superiority, systematics thinking and implementation to act, similar to the concept of science and religion.

- Brahmasutra – the religion: origin, sustenance and dissolution of the world.

- Soldiering: science, skill and art, application in battlefield. (unpublished Brigadier Yudhvir Suri)

7

CONCEPTS SOLDIER RELIGION

Soldier Religion:

Concepts of belief

◈ Belief in one God that does not hurt the humanity.

◈ Reverence of founders of religion that does not cause harmony disturbance.

◈ Status of scriptures that does not produce hatred.

◈ Worship places to discourage fundamentalism.

◈ Prayers and rituals to prevent corrupt Brahmanism and exploit ignorance.

Code of conduct of soldier religion is never discuss religion and related topics that appear critical and negative.

Soldier Religion

Concept of Religion Identity

Soldier has the religious background upbringing identity. Something, emotional sentiment, that is accepted as a part of constitutive identity of the citizen. It is the manifestation of identity accepted as an integral part of the society. This identity strengthens his spirit of fighting for the nation.

Armed forces does not interfere in the religious identity of the soldier but supports to strengthen his spirit of fighting.

Soldier Religion

Concept of brotherhood

Soldier religion is the religion of compassion, love and care. It respects the elders and ancestors. Family units evolve the culture of community and society. Intercommunity marriages are encouraged on the concept of friendship.

Friendship evolves to new relationship. The concept of friendship throughout life as husband – wife prevents break of marriages.

Soldier Religion

Concept of soldier's duty

Soldier has the basic responsibility to fight against the enemy for the national security and integrity.

The concept is strengthened and promoted as "Karma" enshrined in Gita – Sermon of Lord Krishna to Arjun – in Mahabharat war.

Soldier Religion

Concept of incarnation

The concepts of birth, death and rebirth is unique to Indian – born religions. Hinduism, Buddhism, Sikhism and Jainism.

All have accepted the theory of well – placed after – death to the soldier who dies in action on the battlefield.

Soldier religion subscribes to this theory to promote the fighting spirit of the individuals.

Soldier Religion

Concept of religion personal affair

Soldiers have their individual background of religion, personal God, rituals and traditions to worship. Religion and worship remains as the personal affair of each soldier. Army supports the emotional religious sentiments to strengthen the fighting spirit of the soldiers.

Soldier religion evolves in each soldier as he matures in soldiering and way of life.

Soldier Religion

Concept of life

Soldier religion favours the good way of life and contribution to the society.

Vision: Serve the motherland and serve the humanity. Preserve the environment and nature.

Soldier Religion

Concept of woman

Soldier religion has the concept of all women to work. It pronotes their workforce or work – hour economy of the nation.

Army creates employability in Arms and services or civil related administration in organization.

The role of women is based on the principle of Equality, Growth and Economy.

Soldier Religion

Dignity in death

All soldiers aspire dignity in death, that may happen on the battlefield or otherwise.

Soldier religion has the concept that last journey of the soldier should be wrapped with national flag.

It promotes the nationalism spirit in the civil society that penetrates to the younger generation to join the armed forces of the country.

8

RELIGIOUS MEN IN INDIAN ARMY

India has not accepted any faith as a state religion. "Right of freedom" of religion is the constitutional provision articles 25 and 28 that makes India as a secular state. It is further endorsed as the 42nd amendment of the constitution to strengthen this assurance. Article 25 of Indian constitution grants freedom to every citizen of India to profess, practice and propagate his own religion. Further, 42nd permeable of the constitution professes to secure to its entire citizens liberty of belief, faith and worship. Indian Army adopted the constitution of India, therefore, Indian Soldiers remains insulated from politics and religion. Indian Army recruitment is based on merit contrary to reservations in the civil society. Therefore, Indian Army commands respects rather than the vagaries of political conflicts of the present day civil administration.

RELIGIOUS MEN IN INDIAN ARMY

Indian Army has the tradition of "Religious teachers" to its ranks long before independence. It is the use of religion that could be traced to British colonial army. 1857 Indian rebellion against the East India Company (10th May 1857 sepoys mutiny of India) at Meerut garrison tower, resulted execution and imprisonment of hundreds of religious teachers. In the next decade, the colonial military again began to tolerate the religious teachers - Pandits, Granthis, Moulvis in its cantonments infrastructure. In the British Empire, religious traditions of the soldier and the exigencies of service, was give and take system. The religion of the Indian soldier was capable of "assisting or resisting" imperial agendas. It facilitated the loyalty of the soldiers without rebellion. Religious, teachers were tolerated by the administered power in - spite of their dangers. They were the brokers who promised protection, promotion, comfort and miracles to their soldiers. British realized the significance of these religious teachers in the life of soldiers rank and file. Theses religious teachers were accommodated as Junior Commission Officers (JCO's) who could influence the lower ranks and communicate with the military leadership.

Constitution of India denies the soldier to accept personal faith as an individual or in group as the Military religion but soldier is always motivated to use religion as fighting spirit during the war. It is this moral value that facilitates the fighting spirit to victory. The moral value is the battle – cry of each fighting force such as Jai Maa Kaali, (Hindu Gorkhas); Allah hu Akbar, God is great(Muslim soldiers Jammu Kashmir rifles, the Grenadiers Jammu Kashmir light infantry) "Jo Bole So Nihal, Sat Sri Akal," blessed is the one who proclaims the truth of God (Sikh Regiments and Sikh light infantry). Those fighting force units which have mixed caste of sub-units (companies and squadrons) have slogan of "Honour or Izaat," of unity besides the religious war – cry at the time of need.

Militaries, in the countries with officially recognized state religions subordinate their authority to religious Mullas or priest such as Pakistan, Bangladesh, Iran and Israel. In either of these, autonomous or military religion, the fighting spirit is strengthened during the hostile conflict. Military religion is conceptualized as an "institution" and a "social – sphere," where men interact and gain identity. Symbols, identities and values are promoted by the religious teachers in these groups and units. Such religious men are the state sponsored from the religious organizations. This was seen as common traditional authority, that proclaimed in premodern militaries.

Presently, modern military is based on secularism. Recruitment and promotions of the personnel is merit rational legal principles, are governed rather than the religious dictates. However, there are trends of increased religiosity and its permeation to organized societies such as Armed forces (Myanmar, Bangladesh, Pakistan, Iran and Palestine). Deprivatisation of religion (religion no more an individual affair but state sponsored) and desecularization comprises a strengthening of religious elements in the military culture – symbols, ethics and conduct.

Militaries largely mirror the processes that take place in the surrounding civil society, without exception in the affairs of religion. Soldiers' sensitivity to sacrifice is invariable imbued with nationalist sentiments is at a higher level than that in the civil society. Therefore, religious symbols are used as tools to recruit, mobilise and motivate the soldiers.

In post – Vietnam war era US army was influenced of evangelism (preaching of Christianity), the society was religiously diversified and secular. The evangelists (religious teacher) increased their influence within the military, the vacuum created by reduced number of military chaplains provided by the religious organization.

Desecularization empowers the religious and nationalist. Values to encourage the culturally affected ranks of religiously nationalist socialization. This was seen in Israil – Palestinian (Jews non-jews conflict 2008) that promoted the de - secularization of politics.

Conscript militaries reflect religion in the society to a great extant since they are more permeable to religious influences and more committed to tolerating the religious needs of their recruits. Some countries, in particular French Armed Forces, attracted new recruits by social cohesion, equality and religious liberty, that was the need to accommodate the religious soldiers.

- *Roman – Stollman, mediating structures and the military. The case of Religious Soldiers Armed Forces and Society, 2008, 34 (4) 615 - 638*

Religious diversity is strictly adhered in the military units of Indian Armed Forces. Military command attempts to isolate the troops from religious influences that triggers intra – military tensions. Multifaith Indian Army, the command organizes its units around ethnic rather than the religious identities. The military posts religious teachers rather than religiously oriented sponsored chaplains or Mullah. These religious teachers hold the rank of Junior Commission Officer, even if, they are allowed to wear the civilian clothes. They are trained to socialize the soldiers towards religious harmony and adherence to military discipline.

Military religion is not a unified culture. It means an extra - military, pre-existing religion diffused into the military society. It may be interpreted from military view point. It deviates from chaplain religious organizations sponsored church oriented character. It is not exclusively promoted, legitimated, or mediated by one religious organization such as military chaplains. The major benefit is to isolate the military from religious conflicts, as seen in Indian Army.

Religious teachers in the fighting force have restricted themselves to their religious places. It needs to expand the scope of their conduct to the soldiers that would offer psychological support to mitigate fears, traumas and even post-trauma stress disorder (PTSD). This kind of service does not necessarily involve religious issues especially when offered to soldiers of various faiths. Religious teachers should promote an element of healing – healing of communal harmony and healing of wounded soldiers. They should be the healers of **military – religion.**

Prayer, courage and faith are the three dimensions of spirituality. Religion and spirituality are differentiated with razor – blade lines. Spirituality strengthens the psychological support and military Courage Mental support by the religious teacher or associates spiritually elevate the soldiers.

- *Cohen SA Devine service Judaism and Israel's Armed Forces, Farnham, Ashgate, 2013.*

- *Levy Y, Theorising de - secularization of the military _ The US and Isreal Armed Forces and society, 2020, 46 (1) 92 - 115*

Military religion may be defined as an extra – military pre-existing religion diffused into the military society. Religious diversity is strictly adhered to and maintained in the military units. It represent the secular credentials, non-conscript, liberal society. Those religious teachers who support the religious affairs of the soldiers are interfaith independent trained individuals from the civil society to create religious harmony and military discipline. These religious teachers are non-chaplain characters. Prayer and faith strengthen the fighting spirit, courage and mental psychological support to the soldiers.

Religious secularization and privatization are nationalist values of the military religion. It prevents the interfaith conflicts as seen in the Armed Forces India.

Military – religion is known of religiousity with good soldiering, post modernism and liberalism. UK, USA and Israel have documented religious spiritualism to strengthen the identities of nationalism, culture and fighting spirit. It prevents immorality, stress, loneliness, fear and guilt.

- Ramu; Why secularism fails?

  Secular nationalism and religious revivalism in Israel international of politics, culture and society 2008, 21 (1 – 4) 57 – 73.

- *Snape M, God and the British soldier. Religion and the British army in the 1st and 2nd world wars Milton Park, Routledge.*

Who is the authority of military – religion?

Religious military is the "super natural" with, so called, the God. Military in democratic societies with elected civilian governments shape and implement the policies expressing the will of the society as a whole and guided by legal administration. It is the clear unified hierarchy of command from the political authority to the rank and file of Armed Forces. External intervention is intolerant and there is no clash of authority.

Military – religion creates a new category – identity of soldiers that may be extended to the civil society in the long-term. Military religion integrates the young soldier generation to the level of nationalism. Military bias one religion over the other is the privilege to command respect and honor of the soldiers in the civil society.

- *Hassner RE Religion on the battlefield. Ithacal London, Cormel university 2016*

- *Hassner RE Hypotheses on religion in the military International studies reviews 18 (2) 312 – 332.*

- *Access to organizational difficulties of entry into the Armed Forces and the issues related to religion knowledge is significant to the research scholars. However, author of this book Brig. Dr. Yudhvir Suri, VSM is an ex-soldier who served the Engineers and Armoured corps as regimental medical officer and the multifaith Army Medical Corps, India, for almost 35 years.*

- *Levy Y; Military and Religion Department of sociology, political science and communication, open university of Israel, Rananana Israel http//10.1007/978-3-030-02866-4_32-1*

Religion has been the most motivating factor to a soldier for his spiritual and psychological preparation Dharma – Yudhas have been fought to uphold an ideology, territorial expansion, righteousness, communism threatened peace and tranquality.

- Vs Hitler – Mussolini

- Vs Fascist – Nazi

- Vs Leninism – Maxism

- Vs Communism – Bolsheviks Germans

- Vs Christianity Vs Jews Europe

- Vs Japanese cruel graphitization (threatened peace – tranquility)

- Vs American Vs Russians cold war (Evil empire Vs Godless empire)

- Vs communism Cuba, North – Korea, and China

Military scholars monitor the rhythms of peace and war from time to time and predict the next war. New concept of war, "clash of civilization", is anticipated. It is the Christians Vs Muslims, the conflict between them that each community is attempting to dominate the other. How this cyclic recurrence of war precipitate in future is yet to be seen.

Religion and Soldiering:

Army maintains religiously diverse forces by cohesion that is, recruiting from a diverse religious society as it exists today. It surveys the environment across all states which have people from all faith. The soldier is called upon, sometimes, to operate in the conflict-ridden religious society from where the soldier has been recruited. The challenge the religion might pose for the soldier exists but the army relies on the carefully nurtured institutional mechanisms for the soldiers to cope these challenges. Indian soldier defends a state that is constitutionally secular while remaining of strong force of believers. However, it is a challenge to the institution. Soldier is trained to respect every religion, faith, practice, culture and discipline of "Olive – green" uniform. Institutional authority, uniform discipline and religious diversity are the integrated part of the soldiers life and culture.

Religion and soldiering sometimes pose innumerable difficult situations and circumstances. Nation calls its army to a mission and that mission calls for the supreme sacrifice. The job, sometimes, is difficult where uncertainty of mission further create nervous situations. It was seen during the post – independence 1st war

(Kashmir 1947 – 1948) India faced at the Northern border Indian troops were inducted, operations, logistics were exacerbated by religion. Islam was attempted to be exploited by Pakistan. Was the Army then prepared to create a religious cause to effectively counter Pakistan propaganda? The appeal per force had to be the call of the duty, a manifestation of the dharma, as ordained by the individual soldier's faith. A soldiers dharma warranted him to defend those, for whose protection he had been tasked. The spiritual – moral concept of his duty provided him the much needed fearlessness and bravery in the face of extreme dangers to his life and honour of the unit which made the Army rise its Cause. Heroism and martyrs was the time of soldiers. Similar Indian peace keeping force (IPKF) religious dilemma and uncertainty of mission was seen by the Armed Forces during early 1990's.

Soldiers' religion can never be complete if we do not mention, Gita, Lord Krishna and Arjuna. Fear, death, misery of tortured prisoner or wounded battlefield trauma, haunt every soldier fighting a war. Gita document, soldier who is killed in the battle, the soul reaches the heaven – a privilege the extreme yogi enjoys. Earth is promised to him in the event of victory. Military leaders have stated, war should be played as a game, irrespective of its results, victory or defeat. (Gita – Lord Krishna, Rommel, Mansfield, Patton, Fd Marshal Thamaya). Gita document that war is the game but earth belongs to the brave (Veerbhogya – Vasundhara). Napoleon once said, "Death is nothing but to live defeated and inglorious is to die daily."

Indian Army is the volunteer force of more than 1.25 million active soldiers recruited from diverse religiously cultured environment society. Soldiers respect their religion, and that faith becomes the part of multifaith army of the secular India. On joining, a soldier takes oath on the constitution of India and their respective religious scriptures such as Gita, Quaran, Bible to uphold the honour code of the Army. The army celebrate all religious festivals and officers irrespective of their faith and ethnicity participate in all festivals with their soldiers.

Army maintains the places of Worship as Sarv Dharm Sthal on its bases and provides a religious teacher who is supposed to know the religious rituals traditions and customs. Religious teacher remains with the unit during peace and war, accompanies the soldiers to forward fighting field areas.

"Dharma is Karma" duty an honorable duty, of all is the religious slogan of all religions (Gita, Quran, Buddhism, Sikhism, Bible) for the soldiers. Religion is a source of motivation for the soldier in the Army.

- *Ashwani Kumar Dhaliwal BSA soldiers' concept of religion. Journal of Management (50M) Vol 5, (5) 2010, pg 15 – 22 http// www.aeme.com/ IJCIET/indes.asp USSN print 2347 – 3959.*

- *Brar KS; operation blue star. The true story, New Delhi South Asia books, 1993*

- *Mark Tully and Satish Jacob, Amritsar Mrs. Gandhi's last battle, Calcutta Rupa and company, 1985*

- *Ilan Kelman SF, Disaster diplomacy in Jammu Kashmir, International Journal of disaster risk Reduction 2018, p 1 – 9*

MAHABHARAT WAR:

Bharata war (Mahabharat) was fought as the religious theme, righteousness fight against the injustice. It happened in 3137 BC, admittedly Kali - Yug started with the death of Lord Krishna that is 35 years after the war. Kali – Yug calendar has a beginning of 3102 BC; therefore, it is thought that the Mahabharata war took place in 3137 BC. There is a unique description of conversation between the God and devotee. Lord Krishna invokes his spiritual identity at the battlefield to prepare and persuade the wavered Arjuna devotee, the sermon delivered, has been recorded as Gita – the holy book of Hinduism. It is the first reference of warfare diplomacy, strategy, tactics, logistics, weapon of high lethality? Nuclear and medical management of evacuation, transportation and care. It was the war of large army with allies on either side and worked on the rules at the battlefield. After the war, there were only 8 known survivors, Pandavas, Krishna, Satyaki and Yuyutsu. Yudhishthira the eldest of Pandavas estimated 16.60 million dead and 24, 165 missing. Dhrishtadyumna (son of Drupada) was the commander – in – chief of Yudhishthira army from day 1 to 18 whereas Bhishma – pataams (day 1 to 10 days) Dron Acharya (day 11 – 15 day), Karna (day 16 -17), Shalya (day 18) and Ashwatthama (18th night) were the army commanders of the defeated Duryodhana army. Lord Krishna was the manifested divinity, a central player within the Mahabharata narrative, spiritual wisdom to the Pandavas, discourse or conversation between the manifested God and wavered devotee Arjuna at the battlefield, that was recorded, the Bhagavad Gita. Lord Krishna was the charioteer, counselor and guide to Arjana. He is projected as the protector compassion, tenderness and love. He has been an excellent negotiator, a political reformer and preached duty beyond self. He has been a non-combatant in the war, never used the weapons and did not physically participate in the war. He is revered as a supreme architect of Mahabharata and supreme spiritual wisdom to mankind (in the form of Bhagavad – Gita).

9

RELIGIOUS SERVICES ARMED FORCES

RELIGIOUS SERVICE ARMED FORCES:

Traditionally, Cleric – Pandit, Purohit, Priest or Imam - is a representative to administer a religious ceremony to the individual soldier or the military unit.

Chaplain was the term relate to the Christian faith, in recent times, multifaith team concept has gained popularity in military as well as other areas such as healthcare and education.

- *Multifaith [spaces] University of Manchester March 2012 Archieved from original.*

- *Compare Morgan Hugh H (2008). The Etymology of the word chaplain. Chaplain was a member of one institution – a priest of the church serving in another institution – the kings army.*

History document that military Chaplains (priests) were on board proto – naval ships during 8th century BC. Land based religious men (priests) were appointed during the reign of king Edward 1. Later multifaith priests era started during world war 1. Priests were nominated or appointed as commissioned officers trained as soldiers with additional training in faith ceremonies or theological training.

Germans appointed religious priests to the military who had special civilian status without rank structure. However, banned military rabis (priests) during Hitler's reign were reintroduced to the German military on 29th May 2020 with Jewish community of the Armed Forces. Israel defense Forces have a Military Rabbinate Unit that provides religious services to the military personnel, Jewish or non – Jewish. Every military unit or base camp has a military rabbinate personnel assigned responsibility for conducting the religious services. They conduct in the field or peace all related traditions of the soldier's body, identification, post – mortem and military funerals. Military rabbinate units were started in 1948.

Russian empire, army and navy, is documented to have Chaplains since 1914 BC> Ukraine Armed Forces have taken an important role of military Chaplains, those with religious background have volunteered to serve the military units as Chaplains after Russian military intervention. Today Ukraine Chaplain is not an official military position but a volunteer service, many old veterans of World War 2 have joined the Armed Forces.

United Kingdom, Chaplains were priests who were assigned duties other than religious ceremonies such as military engineers or medical care. It had separate Chaplains department in the Army affairs during World War 1 (1919). Chaplain conduct was religious services, spiritual support to the soldiers during peace and war. During World War II, head of Chaplain, in British army was Major General rank, full Colonel and Lieutenant Colonel were the assistant Chaplains. They were commissioned officers and wear uniform. Navy and Airforce had their own chaplain officers. Earlier, Chaplains were from Christianity, Jewish background. Now Buddhist, Hindu, Muslim and Sikh faith Chaplains (priests) have been appointed.

- *Non – Christian Chaplains appointed. BBC news, 19 October, 2005.*

United States of America (USA) military Chaplains have officer rank status with selective promotions. They wear uniform of respective service, Army, Navy and Airforce. They wear cleric attire only during the religious service. Constitutionally USA army has multifaith Chaplain individuals, however, many have promoted Christianity in the free exercise of their religious belief in violation of legal principles. The federal government maintains neutrality of religion and religious affairs. Chaplains have served the United States Armed Forces in the campaigns all over the world and 400 have died.

- *Phillips MM; A Chaplain and an Atheist go to war, The Wall Street Journal, 4 September. 2010.*

- *James Dao Atheists seek Chaplain role in the military. The New York Times, April 2011.*

- *All armies have their insignia of Chaplains and symbols of their respective services.*

Combatant role of Chaplains

The Geneva conventions are silent on whether Chaplains may bear arms. However, the conventions state (Protocol 1, 8 June, 1955, article 43.2) that Chaplains are non – combatants. They do not have the right to participate directly in hostilities. In World War II, Chaplains were unarmed, however, that is the assumption. Chaplains serving in far East were armed.

- *Fraser GM; Quartered safe out here A recollection of the war in Burma. Harper Collins ISBN 0 - 00 – 272687 – 4 Page 109 – 110*

- *Crossby Donald F; Battlefield Chaplains: catholic priests in World War II by Lawerence KS, University Press of Kansas. ISBN 07006 0814 – 1, 1994*

In recent times, Chaplains are not prohibited to bear arms (UK & USA) though, Australia make it an issue of individual conscience captured Chaplains are not considered "Prisoners of war" and must be returned to their home nation unless assigned to minister to the Prisoners of war. Chaplains Medal of Heroism is a special US military decoration, awarded to those who were killed in line of duty. Guerilla war in Iraq, has documented from the material available; that, engineers, medics and Chaplains of the United States Army were the targets "killing doctors and Chaplains was suggested as a means of psychological warfare".

CHAPLAINS – RELIGIOUS PRIESTS IN HEALTH CARE:

Priests may offer spiritual guidance and pastoral care to the patients and their families. It may be individualized to the religious traditions or belief of the community or the region. The concept is to use the "insights" and principles of psychology, religion, spirituality, and theology.

Indian Army, enlisted volunteers, qualified, acharyas, bachelor degree, from different Universities, are selected and trained to benefit the soldiers in war and peace. They are unarmed force to the regiment of their respective faith such as Moulavi's for Muslims, Pandits for Hindus and Granthi's for Sikhs.

They wear uniform but civil attire when at places of worship or religious duties. They take control of those fallen at action during war or religious funeral ceremonies at peace stations. Their presence is always a great consolation to the bereaved families.

Spiritual care in health care has gained importance due to its benefits to the patients and medical professionals. Integrating the skills of spirituality may enhance the ability to communicate with the patients and relatives. It has positive impact on the recovery and well-beings. It gives ability to fight and recover spirituality and medicine is well defined graduation curriculum in USA.

- *(The Association of American Medical Colleges and National Institutes for health care research.)*

- *Puchalski, CM; The role of spirituality in health care: proceedings Baylor University Medical Center 14 (4) 352 – 357*

- *Beaton LB; Koeing R; Religious cognitions and use of prayer. Health and illness, 30 (2) 249 – 253, 1990.*

- *Benson H; Stark M; Timeless healing. The power and biology. New York Scribner, 1996.*

Time of grief or uncertainty or stress motivates the individual to have positivity effect of meditation, faith and prayer. Self - care becomes focal of spiritual and religious support.

Spirituality for health care is applied at three level:

1. **Firstly: decision - making – integrating with identified aggressive interventions that haS resulted reduced mortality.**

2. **Second: Compassionate and holistic care is integrated with spiritual care. It has impact on positive recovery, coping illness and hospitalization, spiritual belief system must be considered as individualized faith.**

3. **Third: Spirituality affectively controls the "stress mediators" in the patients, professionals and health care providers. Spiritual and religious beliefs decrease the exhaustion, burnout syndromes, and depression – anxiety levels.**

The world health organization (WHO) favours four well – being of health such as physical, social, mental and spiritual. It documents religious belief may impact both the positive and negative on health and morbidity. Spirituality is distinct from organized religion. Similarly, definition of spiritualty is understood as an individual's search for meaning and purpose in life. Spirituality is the expanded format of life. One does not need the religious framework, rules, traditions, rituals or the guidelines to be spiritual.

- *Larson JS; The World Health Organization Definition of health. Social versus Spiritual health. Social indicators research 38 (2) 181 – 192, 1996.*

- *Preamble to the constitution of the world health organization as adopted by the international health conference, New York, 19 -22 June 1946 signed by the representative of 61 states (records of WHO No. 2 P 100 and entered into force on 7th April, 1948.)*

Spiritual health within the WHO purview has become significant to consider "Health for All" strategy to motivate people all round aspects of healthy life.

Religiosity mitigates the negative impact of income inequality, injustice on life satisfaction. It is positively associated with mental disorders such as depression, psychotic illnesses, (schizophrenia). One of the best ways to cope with trauma is the concept of religious or spiritual practices. Praying for someone who is sick can have positive effects on the health of the person being prayed. However, there is no change of life expectancy or death rates amongst the people who had religious tendencies except that they had healthier life – style.

- *Joshan 100 M; Weijers D; Religiosity reduces the negative influence of injustice on subjective well – being. A study of 121 Nations. Applied research in quality of life. 11 (2) 601 – 612, 2015*

- *Joshan 100 M; Weijers D; Religiosity moderates the relationship between income inequality and life satisfaction across the Globe. Social indicators research 128 (2) 731 – 750, 2015.*

10

FAITH HEALERS GURU, GURUKUL, DHARAMSHALA CULTURE

FAITH HEALERS OF MANKIND

Dhanvantari

Baba Nanak

Guruji Dugri Wale

In modern military, recruits from the civil society, is shaped to a patriot soldier with the support of experts knowledge and skills of weaponry. These experts were known as "Ustads", so called the instructors at the training regimental centers of arms (infantry, mechanized infantry, artillery, armourd, engineers, etc.) and services (Army service corps, Army medical corps etc.) at different locations in the country. Ancient India Soldiers were trained by the "Gurus" and the modality of training was specific to the status of the individual in the society and his capability. Guru is a Sanskrit word, means a mentor, guide, an expert or master, of knowledge and skill in that field. Guru – Gu, ru. "darkness and light" The guru is seen as the one who dispels the darkness of ignorance. Guru culture in Hinduism has been pan – India, traditionally, a guru as a reverential figure to the disciple. Guru is also a counselor who helps to mould values, shares experiential knowledge, self – example, inspirational source and spiritual evolution to the disciple. The Vedic concepts of Guru evolved as the "Gurukuls" – the education centers, composed holy scriptures (Vedas, Upanishads, Shastras) developed religious institution that preserved the treasure of knowledge, philosophy, art culture and music. It became a tradition of spiritual preceptor of all religions – Hinduism, Buddhism, Jainism, Sikhism.

Soldiers need to study and understand the Bharata war fare. It had celecial and mythological weapons of mass – destruction. It was not only the use of the weapon but the command to neutralize it at the time of need. It appears the technology of advanced missiles system, probably, better than the present day Bhisham Pitamah, Arjun, Drona Acharya and Ashwathama had acquired the knowledge of "innovation and withdrawal" of weapons such as Brahmastra, Narayan Astra, Rudra, Agneya, Vajra etc. Nakul – Sahdev the younger Pandavas had, the expertise of "pain control" of wounded soldiers as physicians Arjun and Drona Acharya were the renowned warriors, Gurgaon, (now Gurugram, 2016) of Haryana was founded as Guru Gram by Drona Acharya on the land given by Dhritarashtra, the king of Hastinapura (now Delhi) in recognition of his teachings of martial arts to the princes, Kauravas and Pandavas. Gurgaon is heritage with reminants of ancient Hindu culture and history of India.

However, Drona Acharya was traditional Guru, son of sage Bhardwaj, decedent of sage Agniras and Parashuram was his mentor Arjun, the winner of Bharata war, was his disciple. Earliest mention of Guru in the Hindu literature is Dhanvantari, the physician of Devas, also identified as great grand-father of Divadasa, a mythological king of Kashi (Varanasi).

Dhanvantari – God of health

Dhanvantari is the God of medicine and worshiped for the well-being of mankind with mantra.

Om Namo Bhagavate, Vasudevaya, Dhanvantraye,

Amrutha Kalasha, Hastaaya Sarva Maya,

Vinashanaya, Trailokya Nathaya, Shri

Mahavishnave, Nameha

Dhanvantari emerged from the Ocean of Milk and appeared with the pot of amrita (elixir of immortality) during the Samudra Manthana, whilst the ocean was being churned by the devas and the asuras, using the Mandara mountain and the serpent Vasuki. The pot of amrita was snatched by the asuras and after this event, Vishnu's avatar, Mohini, appears and takes the nectar back from the asuras.

Nectar is the symbol of immortality in Hindu philosophy and elucidates the role of Dhanvantari in medicine.

According to the Brahma Vaivarta Purana, Dhanvantari, accompanied is disciples, once journeyed to Kailasha. On the way, a naga named Takshaka emitted a venom-spitting hiss. A disciple plucked the diamond the head of Takshaka and hurled it towards the earth. Upon learning events, the powerful serpent-king Vasuki amassed thousands of serpents under the leadership of Drona, Pundarika, and Dhananjaya against the entourage. The poisonous emissions of all these serpents united to make disciples of Dhanvantari faint. Immediately, Dhanvantari concocted medicine made from vanaspati, allowing his followers to recover and causing the snakes to faint in turn. When Vasuki understood what had transpired, he sent a Shaiva serpent goddess, Manasa, to face Dhanvantari. a sent the disciples of Dhanvantari into a swoon, but since the deity was proficient in the art of Vishvavidya, he soon restored his disciples to consciousness. When Manasa deemed it impossible to defeat Dhanvantari disciples, she held the trishula given to her by Shiva and aimed it Dhanvantari. Seeing this, Shiva and Brahma appeared before them and ed the peace, sending them all on their way.

The story document the culture of "Gurukul" in ancient India where disciples were administered knowledge and spirt of various disciplines to numbers of diverse disciples.

There are dedicated temples of Lord Dhanvantari at Kerala, Tamil Nadu, Puducherry, Utter Pradesh, (Varanasi and Haridwar), New Delhi. First Dhanvantari temple has been inaugurated in Rajasthan at Behror (Neemrana – Kotputali belt) of Jaipur.

Dhanvantari temple is also seen at Jaya Bageshware neighborhood of Kathmandu, near Pashupatinath of Nepal.

- *Acknowledge the support of Shri Janak Bahadur Suri, Shri Somesh Bahadur Suri, Shri Munir Suri, to establish Dhanvantari temple at Behror on 10th October, 2024, the auspicious Deshera Day.*

Hindu mythology has advocated healers such as Shiva, Parvati, Dhanvantari, Ashwini Kumaras, and Dharti (solar). It started the concept of holistic (God as a healer) medicine a doctrine of preventive and therapeutic medicine that emphasizes the necessary of looking at the whole-body system – body, mind, emotions, and environment – rather than at an isolated organ function. It is the wide range approach of health care alternative to standard Western medical practices, some scientific or some non – scientific, such as naturopathy, acupuncture, bio feedback homeopathy, psychopathy, nutrition – therapy, yoga message and physical therapy etc. Some groups advocate healing as n integral part of God's character. God cares every area of health, physical, mental, emotional and spiritual. There are experts who invoke, the deities or spirits by tantrism, Jyotish – vidya, and spiritualism for the well – being of the individual. Similarly, Shamanic traditions were known in ancient medicine. It is the process to connect with unseen, energies and nature with altered consciousness. The method may be to lower the barrier of the human conscious, mind and surrender to the spirit reality of nature of the other world. Conscious synereses with the awareness channels of the other world spirits. It connects with the realities and receive information as desired. It is, sometimes, called as psychedelic medicines (external) substances such as music as methods of shamanic therapy. It is the spiritual medicine care, soldiers with back ground from civil society, have the experience and faith, in holistic medicine. In time of stress and isolation, the soldier as per se forced to invoke such methods of selfcare.

14th century was the start of "Dharamshalas" (religious – house) based on the concept to facilitate religion – trade – medical care. Religious saints were the healer to the masses, free langar was served to the poor and the rich, unity of the community was the theme. Traders used these Dharmshalas as travel night halts.

Guru Nanak Dev (15th April 1469 – 22nd September 1539) was an Indian spiritual teacher, mystic poet. He was born at Rai Bhoi ki Talwandi, Nankana Sahib (now in Pakistan) Punjab. The name is thought that he was born in the house of maternal grandparents – "Nankey", Kerma kacha or chotewal, in the district of Lahore. Nanak is said to have travelled far and wide across Asia teaching the masses the message of one God who lives in every one creation and constitutes the eternal truth. It was a unique concept of spiritual, social, political platform based on equality, fraternal love, goodness, and virtue. His teachings in the form of 974 Shabad Lymns have been registered in the holy scripture of Sikhism, the Guru Granth Sahib. He visited Hindu or Muslim pilgrimage centers and preached against to go on a pilgrimage saying that one needs to free the self from maya, evil deeds, and follow the path of righteousness. He said God can be seen in the domestic walls with prayers to salvage of the creator. Each one individual needs to find his own path by renouncing the civil path in the praise of the creator. He debated the religious concepts, tradition, issues with faith promoters Brahmins, Pandits, Mullas, religious teachers across Tibet, South – Asia, Arabia and many ports of the world. Masses joined the movement as it reformed the sick Brahmanism of Hindu culture and adverse Mugalism on the Hindu masses.

His argumentative reforms on the subjects such as God, nature, man, death, rituals, and moral values moved the masses to the new culture of Guruship, Dharmshala culture of Hindu Society. He questioned the sacred thread ceremony at the age of nine years, the Janeu: saying. Do the Brahmin and Kshateriyas lose their faith if they lose their sacred thread. Is their faith maintained by their thread or by their deeds.

Baba Nanak was married to Maa Sulakhni from Batala, had two son Sri Chand and Lakhmi Das but family life did not divert his attention away from spiritualism. He was inducted to materialism with employment under Nawab Daulat Khan at Sultanpur. He served with appreciation of all, the employer and the employees but failed to reconcile, the noose of maya without sowing the seeds of good actions. One can not earn wages without service and it is the love of the wages which stands in the way of renunciation why not then serve the great master, who is the Lord of Universe? Nanak took the decision to devout to the "Will of God to honour and obey the command of the Lord."

Nanak was accompanied by a family Savadar named Mardana, belonged to brewer caste lower community, and was a gifted singer musician. Mardana played the rahab and sang hymns. The faithful Mardana was his sole companion throughout, Nanak preaching. "There is no Hindu, there is no Musalman."

It is interesting that once Nanak observed the crowd bathing in the river and offering water palmful eastward to the Sun. He entered the stream and started throwing water westward. The angry crowd asked why wrong ablation, Nanak, asked the crowd why they offer water eastward to the Sun. they replied:

Where are your dead ancestor's, with the God in heaven?

How far is the abode of the Gods?

Forty – nine crore kos from here.

Does the water get that far?

Without doubt, but why do you throw it westwards?

Nanak said my home and lands are near Lahore. It has rained everywhere except on my land. I am therefore watering my fields.

Man of God how can you water your fields near Lahore from this place?

If you can send water forty – nine crore kos the abode of Gods, I can send it to Lahore which is only a couple of hundred kos away. It impressed the people around and those became disciples to preach against the rituals along with Guru Ji.

Guru Nanak is known to accept the concept of karma. Human birth is the gift of vicious cycle of life, death, rebirth and salvation. Therefore, abolish duality in order to be a complete devotee. Austerity, truth, restrain, and faith in one "Ek Onkar, that is God is one."

Guru Nanak was the healer of the individuals and communities. The manner his body was laid to rest is the testamount of the Hindus and Mussalmans. The dictates of the saint, to place flowers on either side Hindus on right Muslims, on the left. Those flowers remain fresh till tomorrow morning will decide the final way of cremation. Baba Ji went to eternal sleep with chadar over him. Flowers of both the communities remained fresh, both communities celebrated the last rites of the saint. Guru Nanak revered saint of Hindus – Muslims died in the early hours of the morning 22nd September 1539.

Guru Nanak was the 1st Guru of Sikhism but never laid Sikhism as religion, nor advocated a sect of Hinduism. He created mass movement of Hindus – reforms against corrupt, Brahminism and atrocities of Mughals.

Ancestors of Suri Parivar Lala Shivram Das Suri, migrated from Jalalpur Jaitian (now in Pakistan) probably as a result of religious atrocities to the Hindus Maharaja Ranbir Singh of Jammu and Kashmir had opened the doors of those who wanted to migrate to the state in 14th century. Jammu an Kashmir state subject certificates issued by the authorities is the document held by the family.

Dugri wale Guruji – Bade mandir

Guruji, Nirmal Singh Ji Maharaj was born on 07 July, 1952 at Dugri village, near Jalandhar, Punjab. He went to school at Dugri primary school, government high school and Malerkotla college for his graduation. He attained masters degree in English and Economics. He devoted his time mostly to meditate and attracted towards spirituality.

Nirmal Singh Ji worked with Punjab school education board as a clerical assistant in 1983. He travelled to various towns Chandigarh, Panchkula, Delhi and Mumbai, stayed with his devotees and finally settled in Jalandhar. In 1990s, Guruji constructed Shiv Mandir called Bade Mandir in Chatttarpur, Delhi.

Some of the teachings Guruji preached were as under:

- Strike a balance between the duties in this world and the duties towards God. Neither materialism nor the renunciation is the answer of your life.

- Guruji says "Ay Kalyug hai, aide vich rab jaldi mil janda ve. Patha nahin latkana paind." In other words, pray God at your convenience, all with good deeds and good way of life.

- Do not curse or abuse the best to others.

- Brahminism is a curse to the society. Rituals should be discarded, however, the traditions of spiritualism be maintained to remind the individual the culture of the society or civilization.

- Discard the culture of birth – stones, costly jewelry, to avoid the negative influence on your health.

- Discourage waste expenditure on weddings or ceremonies. He is documented to say "Loki ena faltu karcha karde ne vyah utte. Vyah simple hene chahide ne. Asal ceremony kinni jaldi ho jandi hai."

- Guruji preached the concept of God, all religions are one, all God are the same. All religion preach only one language of love, compassion and service to mankind.

- "Never Gossip about another individual sarcastically," they will share your blessings of Karma and you will receive their negativity.

- Money should be thought provoking: "Botta paisa changa nahin honda. Sai itna deejiye jo main kutumb samai," to much money is not good one should have just enough for the family.

Nirmal Singh Ji died on 31 May, 2007, so called attained Maha - Samadhi. Bade mandir, Delhi became the Samadhi Shrine. Navdeep Singh alias Gaurav nephew of Nirmal Singh Ji took over the management of Bade Mandir ashram in the Chattarpur of Delhi.

Guruji started the culture of Sat Sangs, devotees from all parts of India and world came to seek his blessings. The tea and langar Prasad served to the devotees had special Devine blessings. Devotees experienced his grace, the matrix of problems such as legal, financial, emotional were solved, share darshan cured incurable diseases to the individuals. The miracles of blessings to the devotees was the reasons of followers to all sections of the society – ordinary men to most powerful – politician's, businessmen, bureaucrats, armed forces personnel, doctors, engineers, professionals, media and film industry celebrities. Guruji has been the healer of mankind – socio spiritual and the emotional. He never delivered speeches or sermons nor prescribed the black magic rituals. It was his connection with the devotee, that transformed the life of the devotee to a level where joy, fulfillment and peace was granted. It has been a unique phenomena of spiritualism.

- Sat Sang: assembly of persons, with company of the highest truth, Guruji who listen to, talk about and assimilate the truth.

Guruji is no more in mortal guise, however, his blessings are working the same wonders with his grace, falling on the devotees who never met him in their lifetime. Sat Sang is the medium to meet Guruji.

The purpose of Nirmal Singh Ji, as documented, during his lifetime, and after-life has been to deliver the humanity of illness disease and suffering. People thronged to Guruji, even today, for deliverance of problems, may be health, job, disease, business, money that had latched on them due to their Karma. He was an embodiment of the divine for the love of millions of people. He wished his devotees to become good human beings, citizens were given the message to help everybody, elevate the Karmic life with good deed, behaviour and non – materialism.

Nirmal Singh Ji, preached the message:

Awwal Allah Noor upaaya

Kudrat ke sab Bande

Ek Noor Te Sab Jag upjaye

Kaun Bhale Kaun Mande

India is blessed with the presence of enlightened personalities from ancient time till to date. These Mahapurush's Saints, Seers, faquirs belonged to Hinduism, Buddhism, Sikhism, Islam and even Sufi culture. They had the power to invoke, nurture and protect the civilization. It sustained faith of the individuals and the society to Dharma. Guruji was an embodiment of the Divine, Mahapurush of the present time Guru, as the word suggests, removes the darkness of ignorance. He attains pedestal higher than that of God:

Gurur Brahma

Gurur Visahnu

Gurur deva Maheshwarah

Gurur Sakshat parbrahm

Tesmey Shri Gurve Namah

The holy trinity of God - Brahma, Viashnu, Shiva – the power of Guru is limitless. He is creator, preserver, resurrector (Maheshwarah) and absolute God (Parbrahm).

Fortune prediction is an art and, sometimes, science of astrology, palmistry and horoscope amongst the saints and seers. Guruji

Nirmal Singh Ji predicted the misfortunes of the individuals with "face contact" and immediately resolved to benefit the persons. He cured diabetes, malingancy, cancer, coronary block heart disease, neurological disorders such as prolapse discs and neurolgias, myopathies, depression, anxiety, emotional disorders, and child birth to women. It was spiritualism to the benefit of masses. It was not only the predicted problem, resolution spontaneously but resolution relief was proved with advance medical technology of modern time.

- *Light of divinity, 3rd edition, 2010, www. Gurujimaharaj.com (for private circulation only)*

- *While the divine father blessed us with son, accidents averted on road and tarmac, saved in flooded Mumbai Pg 16 – 26 The healer in white clothes Pg 39 - 42*

- *Six years after marriage I conceived Pg 51 - 52*

- *Guruji saves my marriage Pg 57 – 58*

- ***The divine healer treats the doctors by Brig. Dr. Saini consultant AHRR Delhi.***

- *Guru Kripa by Dr. Chandrekant S Pandav, HOD community medicine, N Delhi.*

- *Many miraculous years with Guruji by Lieutenant Colonel D S Chatterjee, Siemans.*

- ***Man of medicine bows to faith by Dr. Inder Mohan Bhatia, AIIMS New Delhi***

- *In Him Lives the Jyoti of Lord Shiva by justice AS Gill former High Court Judge.*

- ***A Soldier Salutes Guruji by Lieutenant General CK Kapoor, PVSM, AVSM.***

- *A lady is healed at Bade mandir Pg 239*

- *A healing current passed through my arm Pg 240*

- *Alcoholism spirited away Pg 265 – 267.*

- *Master of life and death Pg 273 – 286*

- *"I am Shiva, I am everything." Guruji proclaimed his identity…. "you need not go anywhere else because I am God" by Narinder Dhand*

- *Depression disappears on hearing Guruji Pg 325*

- *Operation in dream rids wife of heart ailments Pg 386 SK Behl*

- *Guruji pours water over advanced cancer – ovarian malingnancy by Narinder Taneja Pg 287 – 289.*

The above statements are a few from the large documented saviour of sufferings of humanity. **One thing is clear, that, Sat Sang culture has become the mass movement in the society.** People visit Bade Mandir or designated Sat Sang to have darshan of Guruji – that mitigates their sufferings and fulfill their desires of good healthy way of life. Passionate love or divine, has been the devotional Bhakti movements, that stresses the mystical union of the individual with God. Bhakti movement developed between 7th and 12th century. It was Shaivities and Vaishnaite culture that preached personal God devotion as a means of salvation. Saints Kabir, Guru Nanak, Tulsidas, Chaitanya, Mira – bai, Adi – Shankaracharya have united the civilization with mass movements. Later the socio political leaders Mahatma Gandhi, Vinoba – Bhave created the mass movement but that was more on the theme of freedom of India. **Guruji Nirmal Singh Ji mass movement has been unique in two respects, firstly, to "mitigate the sufferings" secondly "good way of life" spiritualism is the means to alleviate the sufferings.** It is not the union of the individual with God, as seen, during the Bhakti movement of ancient India.

The concept of the Nirmal Singh Ji Guruji mass movement is equality, social participation, Nirguna (beyond attributes of God) Sufi – Vaishniaism, personal experience with God (God as formless, non

– incarnate, ethereal, ineffable, though, it may use different names). Some devotees visualized him as Shiva or document Guruji identity as Shiva reveals single God concept, the supreme Maheshwara. Those who have visited the Bade Mandir may realize that the concept is centred around Sikhism (Guru Nanak) Shivaism (Lord Shiva), compassion love and care. Non – ritual, non – idol, non – pilgrimage, non – wasteful ceremonies are the highlights. Serve the nation, serve the society, charity and social work have been adopted from the saints such as Swami Viveka Nanda and Mahaprabhu.

Soldier is a product of society trained to serve the national security and integrity. He has an identity different than the civilian citizen of the country. He is not easily influenced by the mass movements of religious nature. He is hard – trained to respect his religious back – ground, to care the religious sentiments of comaradie, adopt and evolve the new religion called the soldier religion. Still he remains open to the external influences at the time of stress and likely to visit the spiritual Gurus as seen here large number of defense forces, officers and men.

Myself, Brig. Dr. Yudhvir Suri, is a medical practioner and scientist of medicine, does not undermine the spiritualism cure of medicine but fails to reconcile the cure of malignant diseases, coronary heart block (as seen on angiography) respiratory infections (rescued from intensive care units). Soldier religion supports the spiritualism but not the fundamentalism.

ABOUT THIS BOOK

Did we miss the history of military medical leaders? Yes, they were contributors to excellence, walked on rough pebbles road, paved the way of future generation to deliver medical care to the soldiers. Those who took over the Patanjali empty bowls, handed over the Dhanvantari nectar - full bowl of immortality health to the soldiers. (Immortality denotes here strong, healthy soldiers of future generation). They never stopped their foot forward to achieve the highest rank and position with professionalism at Indian Military Medicine.

Stress, spirituality, religion and health are interrelated to mitigate psychological, emotional, mental and physical well-being. Stress coping framework facilitates social and emotional support, hope and optimism, perception of control to self, behavioural change, decreases fear and insecurity. It regulates the effects of stress on negativity and lifestyle medical disorders. High spiritual well-being scale is associated with low incidence of depression, psychosis, negative emotions, conflicts and mental disorders.

Stress may be beneficial to promote adaptability, to overcome crisis, increase performance productivity and revenue. It facilitates life-style. It promotes the cognitive-equity concept to create inclusive environment. Human body has inbuilt system to cope with the phenomenon of stress called General Adaptation Syndrome (GAS). However, stress should never be stretched to the level of exhaustion, General Adaptation System fails, that deteriorates the body responses to adverse outcome. One needs to understand the level of stress to the level of exhaustion.

Combat stress, denial does not evaporate the ground reality. Soldering is stressful and evidence exists that stress consequences are seen on the Indian soldiers. All armies over the world have admitted that their soldiers have suffered Combat Fatigue Syndrome. It took 120 years to reach the consensus diagnosis, specific syndrome, in individuals who experienced major life events.

There has been perplexity in diagnosis, denial to accept the clinical medicine, label the soldier as malingerer, administer the death warrant and execution on orders of military command. Perplexity also existed on modes of extreme management, declaring the soldiers unfit or placing them to frontline psychiatric unit hospitals. American psychiatry association (1980) accepted combat stress as the acute reaction and post traumatic stress disorder as the delayed reaction among the soldiers exposed to the combat. Forward combat psychiatry management prevents the delayed manifestations of the disease.

Do we need religion in Armed Forces? Yes, religion is the thought concept relevant to the Armed Forces in fighting spirit, if that fails, the cause of devotion fails. The need of the religion is devotion to the cause and that cause is existence of the Armed Forces

Each religion has a doctrine, worship, uniqueness and individuality of its own. It changes in response to the needs of the age or time. Then why not to have the doctrine of soldier-religion. It is the fellowship of the soldier's spirit, experience, humanity, and humanitarian common essence of mankind.

Man's evolution is bound with his conscious deeds. Those who have evolved, excel in their talent, skills and deeds, become exemplary to others, sometimes, penetrate to become history. That is what happens to the soldier, a patriot from the citizen.

Religion teaches us to attain the highest mode of experience - what soldier desires the ultimate experience of soldiering? To win the war or defeat the enemy.

Soldier is a new religion. It is a social integrity that develops in the barracks and training grounds of those who have variable background of caste, creed, belief, traditions, culture, language, rituals, personal god and way of life. It is the way of life, care and concern, simple thought, Nation first and nationalism.

The five pillars of religion are transformed to the upbringing of the soldier:

1.   Belief in God: that does not hurt the humanity.

2.   Reverence of founders: of the religion that do not produce hatred.

3.   Scriptures: that did not cause harmony disturbances.

4.   Worship places: to discourage fundamentalism.

5.   Rituals: to prevent exploitation of ignorance (Brahminism).

The Code of Conduct of soldier - religion, is never discuss religion, the topics that appear critical and negative. One God, creator, preserves and destroyer, omniscient, omnipotent and omnipresent, benign and merciful to the faithful is admitted as the soldier's religion.

Modern military of India, is based on secularism. Recruitment and promotions of the personnel is merit rational legal principles, are governed rather than the religious dictates. Religious diversity is strictly adhered in the military units of the Indian Armed Forces. Military command attempts to isolate the troops from religious influences that triggers intra-military tensions.

Religious services are provided to the soldier by qualified religious teachers. Indian army, enlisted volunteers, qualified acharyas, bachelor degree, from different Universities, are selected and trained to benefit the soldiers in war and peace. They are unarmed force to the regiment of their respective faith such as Moulavis for Muslims, Pandits for Hindus and Granthis for Sikhs. They take control of those fallen at action during war or religious funeral ceremonies at peace stations.

Indian military medicine suggest to expand the scope of religious teachers to offer psychological support to the soldiers to mitigate fears, trauma and even post-trauma stress disorders. They should promote an element of healing - healing of communal harmony, healing of wounded soldiers. They should be the healers of the military - religion.

Faith-healers of mankind have appeared in the civil society in the past and will appear in future. It is the personal belief of the individuals as spiritual relief. Soldier - religion does not support the mortal - guise spiritual guru concept.

BRIGADIER YUDHVIR SURI, VSM

Brigadier Yudhvir Suri, VSM:

Author

Academician, Researcher, Cardiovascular and thoracic anesthesiology critical care clinician; served Armed forces, Army Medical corps India.

Brigadier Yudhvir Suri was a military doctor, Army Medical Corps, Armed forces India, born in Lahore pre-partition India on 07 April 1945. He graduated medicine from government medical collage Srinagar Kashmir in 1967 and decided to join Armed forces medical Services India in January 1968. He served the soldiers as Regimental Medical officer during 1971, India-Pakistan war at chhamb-Jaurien western border of Jammu-Kashmir. He volunteered his choice speciality of medicine Anesthesia at Armed forces Medical college Pune 1972. He qualified Armed forces Board Examination with strenuous training at AFMC and command hospital, lucknow as a "graded" specialist of Army

Medical corps, Armed forces India in 1974 and doctorate medicine Anesthesiology (MD Anesthesiology) from Pune University in 1975 Graded specialist, Armed forces medical service has the system of training the medical graduates to various disciplines of medicine that is needed to serve the soldiers with standard curriculam education and examination, Board of examiners certify the candidate as a "graded specialist" who can administer the specialist to the soldiers, even without university diploma or degree. It fullfills the needs of the Armed forces India and acceptable to Medical council of India, the standards of Medical Education.

Brigadier Yudhvir Suri served military soldiers during war and peace at various military hospitals and simultaneously participated educational "forums in civil teaching medical institutes, discussions and conferences.

As a result he became a recognised personality of Anesthesiology. He published more than 200 research papers in reputed medical Journals to identify himself as an academician of medical field. His experimental animals research on short-acting non-depolarising muscle-relaxant chandonium, iodide alongwith professor (Dr) BN Dhawan scientist director at Central Drug Research Institute Lucknow India, till the final human phase III and phase IV clinical trials, has placed him as aclaimed Medical Research Scientist. He was granted Doctorate of philosophy in Medicine (Anesthesiology) Phd under the guidance of well known medical teacher Prof. AM Deshpande of BJ medical college Pune, by the university of Pune Maharashtra in 1994.

In 1985, Brigadier Yudhvir Suri was the first army doctor anesthesiologist to join the field of super-speciality under the guidance of professor head Dr. GR Gode at All India Institute of Medical Sciences, new Delhi, joined Panangpali Venugopal head, Cardiovascular Surgery for advance training in cardiovascular and thoracic anesthesia and administered more than 100 open heart surgeries. During this period, Brigadier Yudhvir Suri was Instrumental to initiate along with Professor HL kaul, associate professor, anesthesiology, the Journal of

Anesthesiology-clinical pharmco-logy as the founder editors of the Journal, aclaimed to be one of the best Journals of Anesthesiology in the world. He was the first institutionalised trained cardiovascular thoracic anaesthesiologist to be posted at Sciences of Cardiovascular and thoracic Institute, affiliated to Armed Forces Medical College, Pune.

Sciences, skill and techniques of well trained anaestesiologists facilitated the growth and patient care of the cardiovascular thoracic Surgery. During the period Armed Forces Medical research Committee sponsored projects were undertaken to develop the new concepts and techniques in management of open heart surgery.

1990-1993, the peak militancy period in Kashmir, he managed 3000 trauma patients with zero mortality. First time in military medicine he developed the concept of Golden Hour management of militancy trauma critical care. His innovative skills of management of penetrating and non penetrating cardiac militancy trauma saved many lives. Critical management of largest 99 number of maxilla-facial injuries during the period has been reported in military medicine. President of India honoured him with Vishisht Seva Medal (VSM) to recognise his distinguished service of a high order in 1995. He also received General officer commanding-in-chiefs (Goc-in-c) "The commendation award" for act of distinguished service and for devotion to duty in 1994.

Brigadier Yudhvir Suri was awarded prestigious Rukamani Pandit Gold-medal by Indian Society of anesthesiologists for research "Animal and Human toxicity of Intravenous anaesthetic Etiomidate, an accidental finding during animal experiments at central drug Research Institute Lucknow India in 1982. He was solicited by Director General Armed Forces Medical Services for best paper award at Armed Forces Medical College in 1992. He was elected president of International Trauma anaeshiesia India, society of anesthesiology-clinical pharmacology, honoured by military and civil societies. Anesthesiology bestowed respect honour and dignity to his life.

Post-retirement he settled at Gurugram (12, 2017) Contributed writing and publishing religious, socio-economic, socio-political, concerns of the soldier and military medicine.

- The Story of: Doctor-soldier, Auto-biography. Published by vasudha, 18th 19th (special issue) vol 5, 2018.

- War Medical Heros: Regimental Medical officer; Vasudha, 26th issue Vol 6, 2021

- Partition of Indian Army: Birth of failed Pakistan Armed forces Vasudha, 11th issue, vol 3, 2017.

- Service by Army Medical Corps to soldier by Brigadier Yudhvir Suri, Vasudha, 28th issue, 2022.

- Military medicine super high altitude, impact on health of soldier, 2023.

- Indian military medicine, volume 2, 2024

His passion for research and writing is the result of this book: Soldier stress: Spirituality and religion, religious men in Indian army and Concepts of soldier religion.

Brigadier Suri is an acclaimed expert on military medicine.